St Antholin's Lectureship

Charity Lecture 2012

Gospel Trials in 1662:
TO STAY OR TO GO?

Peter Adam

Gospel trials in 1662: to stay or to go? © Peter Adam 2012

ISBN   978-1-906327-13-2

With the exception of the translations on pp. 52 and 55 which are the author's own, all scripture quotations are taken from THE HOLY BIBLE, NEW INTERNATIONAL VERSION®, NIV® Copyright © 1973, 1978, 1984 by Biblica, Inc.™ Used by permission. All rights reserved worldwide.

Cover photo © brozova - Fotolia.com

Published by the Latimer Trust September 2012

CONTENTS

1. Preface

My thanks to the St Antholin's Lecture Trustees for the invitation to write and give this Lecture, and to the Latimer Trust for publishing it.

I am grateful to Lee Gatiss for encouraging me to tackle this topic, and for helpful suggestions from Lee, Rhys Bezzant, Tim Patrick, and Mike Flynn. And I deeply grateful to those whose have done the primary work of research which I have used. I hope that this introductory overview will help more people understand the past, and especially what happened to the church of Jesus Christ in England in 1662, and the significance of those events.

I am thankful too for the resources available in the Ridley Melbourne Library, and the Dalton McCaughey Library.

As I have prepared this lecture, I have been reminded again of the faithful gospel witness and outreach of St Antholin's Church, which was one of the first churches in London to adopt the Reformation. It became a centre of gospel ministry, with a ministry of training preachers and expanding ministry to other churches around England. I praise God for the godly ministers and people of St Antholin's.

This lecture is dedicated to the saints of 1662 who endured the gospel trials of that time, including those who stayed within the Church of England for the sake of Christ and the gospel, and those who left the Church of England, for the sake of Christ and the gospel. They honoured God by enduring those trials, and by their lives and ministries. May their examples encourage us to fight the good fight, keep the faith, and run the race, so that we, with them, may receive the crown of righteousness from the Lord Jesus Christ at his appearing.

2. What happened in 1662?

1662 was a defining year for the church in England, and for the Church of England. After a time of religious and political turmoil, a resolution was achieved, which had long-term effects on Christianity in England, and eventually on Christianity throughout the world.

After the death of the Lord Protector Oliver Cromwell in 1658, the Commonwealth collapsed. This collapse of political power had far-reaching results, not least for Christians, for churches, and for gospel ministry in England.[1] Charles II was welcomed home as king in 1660, and Episcopacy, Anglican practice and the *Book of Common Prayer* and the *Thirty-Nine Articles* were restored to the Church of England between 1660 and 1662. Ministers were required to subscribe to the Act of Uniformity of May 1662, and to use the 1662 *Book of Common Prayer*.[2] The date set for this subscription and conformity was St Bartholomew's day, 24th August 1662. About 936 ministers did not conform, and so left ministry in the Church of England, and many more had left since 1660 for similar reasons. Those who left were Puritans, who held to rigorous Reformed doctrine and practice. In total 1760 ministers left the Church of England between 1660 and 1662, about 20% of its clergy. These included Rectors and Vicars, Curates, Parish Lecturers (i.e. Preachers), Schoolmasters, and University Fellows and Lecturers.[3]

Samuel Pepys attended St Dunstan's Fleet Street to hear Dr Bates' farewell sermons on Hebrews 13:20-22 to crowded congregations on Sunday 17th August, and commented, 'I pray God

---

[1] Gerald R. Cragg, *Puritanism in the period of the Great Persecution 1660-1688*, (Cambridge: Cambridge University Press, 1957), pp. 1,2.

[2] An electronic copy may be found at: http://www.churchofengland.org/prayer-worship/worship/book-of-common-prayer.aspx

[3] A.G. Matthews, *Calamy Revised*, (Oxford: Clarendon, 1988 {1934}), pp. xii, xiv.

keep peace among us and make the Bishops careful of bringing in good men in their room, or else all will fly a-pieces; for bad ones will not [go] down with the City'.[4] Richard Baxter was an eminent minister who had been ordained as an Anglican, but decided that he could not conform. He wrote of this St Bartholomew's day,

> When Bartholomew day came, about one thousand eight hundred or two thousand ministers were silenced and cast out...And now came in the great inundation of calamities which in many streams overwhelmed thousands of godly Christians, together with their pastors...[5]

This was a most significant event for those involved, for the Church of England, and for the progress of gospel ministry in England. It profoundly changed the Church of England, led to intense persecution of those who had not conformed and of their followers, and created 'nonconformist' churches which have continued until this day. It had a profound effect on Anglican identity, English identity, and Christian identity in England, and on the way the English people perceived Christianity.

King Charles himself seemed to want a broader Church, which would have included many who later resigned, especially the Presbyterians, whose leaders had worked for his return. His *Declaration of Breda* included a declaration of 'a liberty to tender conscience'.[6] The *Worcester House Declaration* of 1660 promised toleration, and prominent Puritans including Edward Reynolds, Richard Baxter and Edward Calamy were offered Bishoprics.[7] The 1660 Act of Confirming and Restoring Ministers restored

---

[4] Samuel Pepys, *The Shorter Pepys*, [ed.], Robert Latham, (London: Folio, 1985), p. 219.

[5] Richard Baxter, *The Autobiography of Richard Baxter*, N.H Keeble [ed.], (London: Dent, 1974), p. 175.

[6] Gerald Bray [ed.], *Documents of the English Reformation*, (Minneapolis: Fortress Press, 1994), p. 545.

[7] See I.M. Green, *The Re-Establishment of the Church of England 1660-1663*, (Oxford: Oxford University Press, 1978), pp. 143-154.

ministers who had been removed from office in 1645, when the *Book of Common Prayer* had been abolished by the Commonwealth. It removed Baptist ministers, but allowed Presbyterians to continue. However the Savoy Conference of 1661, which included Bishops and prominent Puritans, achieved nothing,[8] and Bishop Sheldon and the Convocation of the clergy of the Church of England had a narrower Church in mind. Sheldon, later Archbishop of Canterbury, said that, 'If we had thought so many of them would have conformed, we would have made it straighter [i.e., narrower]'.[9] The 1662 Act of Uniformity required episcopal ordination, which had not been available since 1645, and had not previously been required for ministers from Continental Reformed churches.[10] It required 'unfeigned assent and consent to all and to everything contained and prescribed' in the *Book of Common Prayer*, even though copies of that Book were not available until a few days before 24th August, and the Book itself was not officially approved until December. It also required subscription to the *Thirty-Nine Articles*, renunciation of the Solemn League and Covenant, and subscription to the notion that it was not legal to take up arms against the King or to attempt change of government in either church or state.[11]

As we have seen, about 20% of the clergy resigned by

[8]   A. Harold Wood, *Church unity without uniformity: A Study of Seventeenth Century English Church Movements and of Richard Baxter's Proposals for a Comprehensive Church*, (London: Epworth, 1963), p. 210. See also, Gerald R. Cragg, *From Puritanism to the Age of Reason: A Study of Changes in Religious thought within the Church of England 1660-1700*, (Cambridge: Cambridge University Press, 1966), pp. 170-224.

[9]   As quoted in Wood, *Church unity*, p. 22.

[10] In fact 465 of those who resigned had been episcopally ordained, so resigned for other reasons. See Wood, *Church unity*, pp. 229, 232.

[11] John Spurr, 'From Puritanism to Dissent 1660-1700', in Christopher Durston and Jacqueline Eales, [eds.], *The Culture of English Puritanism 1560-1700*, (Houndmills: Macmillan, 1996), pp. 234-265. The quotation is on p. 237.

refusing to subscribe, (although of these 170 later conformed).[12] Their reasons varied. Some did not want to accept the authority of Bishops, or wanted Diocesan Bishops replaced by local Bishops with reduced powers. Some objected to the words of the 1662 *Book of Common Prayer*, or to the fact that they had not been able to see it before they were required to subscribe, or that the level of acceptance required was too high. Others would have used the book, but wanted the freedom to use other prayers in church especially extempore prayers. Some objected to being re-ordained.[13] Some objected to elements in the *Book of Common Prayer* that were not commanded by Scripture, and to being required to accept and practice merely human ideas. Richard Baxter objected to the diminished rights of ministers in pastoral decisions and church discipline.[14] John Oldfield, of Carsington, decided that he could not conform only after long and serious consideration. He objected to re-ordination. He imagined a parishioner saying to him, 'If you were no minister before, why did you exercise that function? ...If you were indeed a minister, why do you now seek a new commission?'[15] Such an act would bring into question his previous ministry.[16] The moderate Presbyterian John Howe refused to conform because he believed that the 'terms of communion' of a Church should be no narrower than those of Christianity, and that

---

[12] John Spurr, *The Post-Reformation: Religion, Politics and Society in Britain 1603-1714*, (Harlow: Pearson Longman, 2006), p. 147.

[13] Bishops had been abolished in 1645, so all those who had been ordained since then had not received Episcopal ordination.

[14] Wood, *Church unity*, pp. 214-222, 258. This had been a recurring issue for Puritans. See Peter Ackroyd, 'Strangers to Correction: Christian Discipline and the English Reformation', in Lee Gatiss, [ed.], *Preachers, Pastors and Ambassadors, The St Antholin's Lectures, Volume II, 2001-2010*, (London: The Latimer Trust, 2011), pp. 123-148.

[15] Iain Murray [ed.], *Sermons of the Great Ejection*, (London: Banner of Truth, 1962), pp. 166,167.

[16] Murray, *Sermons*, p. 167.

any greater restriction was a sin.[17]

This significant number of resignations and deprivations should be seen in the light of the 3000 Anglican clergy who resigned or were deprived by the Commonwealth Long Parliament in August 1645, when the use of Prayer Book was forbidden, the Directory of Public Worship imposed, and the Bishops finally removed from office.[18] This was its precedent, and 1662 was an understandable response to 1645. While 1662 looked like intolerant injustice, so did 1645, whatever the quality of the ministers who were deprived or who resigned in either situation.

In fact, during the Commonwealth many were able to attend Anglican services.[19] Even in the days of the Commonwealth, 300 Episcopal Puritans (called 'Evangelicals' by a contemporary writer) had met regularly in Oxford for Anglican worship.[20] John Evelyn's diary makes it clear that he was able to join in services of the *Book of Common Prayer* during the Commonwealth.

One difference between the two events was that in 1645 the Commonwealth allowed dispossessed Anglican ministers a pension of one fifth of their stipend, whereas there was no financial provision for nonconformists in 1662. Bishop Hensley Henson wrote, 'The Anglican of the Restoration was a religious persecutor inspired by political panic, the Puritan of the Commonwealth was a persecuting social reformer inspired by religious fervour'.[21]

---

[17] David P. Field, *'Rigide Calvinisme in a softer dresse': The Moderate Presbyterianism of John Howe, 1630-1705*, Rutherford Studies in Historical Theology, (Edinburgh: Rutherford House, 2004), pp. 54-63.

[18] Owen Chadwick, *The Reformation*, (Harmondsworth: Penguin, 1972), pp. 244,245.

[19] Robert S. Bosher, *The Making of the Restoration Settlement: The Influence of the Laudians: 1649-1662*, (Westminster: Dacre Press, 1951), pp. 10-13. The situation was less congenial after 1655, see p. 41.

[20] V.H.H. Green, *Religion at Oxford and Cambridge*, (London: SCM, 1964), p. 147.

[21] As quoted in Wood, *Church unity*, p. 232.

Of those who left between 1660 and 1662, some, like Thomas Manton, Philip Henry, and Richard Baxter, continued as members of the Church of England, though not as its ministers.[22] Baxter's stated aim was 'to separate from them no further than they separate from God.'[23] They continued to attend their parish church and encouraged their followers to do the same, while also providing supplementary teaching and pastoral care to them. Some set up secret churches. Around fifty were appointed Chaplains to households.[24] All who set up any form of public or private meeting, or who took part in such meetings faced persecution, including fines, loss or property, and imprisonment. While in the years that followed Charles II attempted to make the Church more comprehensive, the Parliament increased the pressure on nonconforming ministers and people alike, with the File Mile Act of 1665, and the Conventicle Acts of 1664 and 1667. In the words of Diarmaid MacCulloch,

> This was a persecution of Protestants by Protestants unique in Europe in its intensity and bitterness: another major question-mark against the complacent English boast of a national history of tolerance.[25]

To which we might add, that it also questions the complacent Anglican boast of a history of tolerance!

The 1672 Declaration of Indulgence provided some relief, and ministers were relieved of the penalties of the 1662 Act if they agreed to those of *The Thirty-Nine Articles* that did not include references to Bishops, and if they registered themselves and their

---

[22] Spurr, 'Puritanism to Dissent', p. 241.
[23] Quoted in Wood, *Church unity*, p. 242.
[24] Green, *Re-Establishment*, p. 163, and see J.T. Cliffe, *Puritans in Conflict: The Puritan Gentry during and after the Civil Wars*, (London and New York: Routledge, 1988), p. 195.
[25] Diarmaid MacCulloch, *Reformation: Europe's House Divided 1490-1700*, (London: Penguin, 2004), p. 531.

buildings. About 1508 ministers registered under this provision.[26] Later there was some Anglican support for a more comprehensive settlement, led by high-church clergy including Archbishop Sancroft.[27] The loss of Sancroft and the Nonjurors on the accession of William and Mary in 1689 meant that a more comprehensive church was not achieved.[28] Instead the Act of Toleration of 1689 allowed relief from penalties for Trinitarian and Protestant nonconformists. The number of their meeting-houses increased from 939 in 1690 to 1257 by 1710. A number of effective Dissenting Academies were founded to train nonconformist ministers.[29] Nonconformists were not allowed to graduate at universities until the 19th Century, and the Church of England still remains the established church.

---

[26] Norman Sykes, *From Sheldon to Secker: Aspects of English Church History 1660-1768*, (Cambridge: Cambridge University Press, 1959), p. 75

[27] Sykes, *Sheldon*, pp. 82-89.

[28] The Nonjurors believed that their promise to serve King James II could not be transferred to William and Mary. They were expelled from the Church.

[29] Sykes, *Sheldon*, pp. 91-104.

3. Why did it happen?

Cause and effect are notoriously difficult to identify, especially from the distance of 350 years. And human motivation is even more difficult to identify, because people do not always explain the reasons for their actions, and the same action may have a variety of motivations. Even if we could ask people why they acted as they did, we could not trust their answers. And of course, with our modern hermeneutic of psychological, sociological or political suspicion, we may attribute different motivations than those claimed by those involved! And Christians have always known that sin blinds us in regard to our actions and motivations.

Furthermore, while it is tempting to separate out, for example, religious, political, personal and cultural causes, it is not possible to do so. We may distinguish a cause as primarily religious, or primarily political, but separation is impossible.

While we cannot be certain of cause and effect, or of human motivations, here are some of the contexts for what happened, and reasons commonly suggested for this mass resignation, this ejection of so many ministers.

3.1 Puritan political instability

Puritanism was widely associated with political instability from the start of the Civil War in 1642. This included the Civil War, the execution of Charles I, the political conflict and instability of the Commonwealth, and the failure to provide effective and acceptable government without a King. The Commonwealth had seen various forms of government, none of them effective or acceptable. Despite the rhetoric of democracy, this experiment failed, with government successively provided by the Rump Parliament, the Barebones Parliament, then by Cromwell the Protector and Parliament, and then by Cromwell and the Army, with Cromwell gaining kingly rights and privileges. There was continuing conflict between the

Army and civilian officials.[1]

The Puritan colonies in New England in America in this period were also marred by political conflict. Should all have the vote, or only believers, or believers and their children? What authority did the state have in religious issues? What place did Baptists have in Congregationalist colonies? Should churches have Congregationalist or Presbyterian polity? How should state and church deal with religious nonconformists?[2]

So the death of Oliver Cromwell left a political vacuum, with no strong desire to continue that form of democracy. It had not worked, and lacked credibility. The obvious alternative was to return the monarchy.

Significantly, Puritan Presbyterians helped this to happen, as of course did those who still valued the old Church of England. Political stability had previously been expressed in monarch and church: one King and one Church were the keys to this stability. And the close connection between monarch and church was of a product of the Reformation, with the monarch taking over the role of the Pope, and becoming the Head of the Church. In fact the role of the monarch had changed, as it was Parliament who invited Charles II to return, but at least the appearance echoed the past. In the words of Gerald Cragg, 'The Restoration took place because the majority of Englishmen were weary of experiments and wanted to return to familiar ways.'[3] And as anti-popery was a political not a religious stance, so too anti-Puritanism was political, not primarily religious. In the words of a Tory poem, 'Rome and Geneva both strive to pull down/the envied mitre and imperial crown'.[4] The trial

[1] Spurr, *Post-Reformation,* pp. 126-130.
[2] Francis J. Bremer, *The Puritan Experiment: New England Society from Bradford to Edwards,* (London: St James Press, 1976), pp. 57-71, 89-105, 125-126.
[3] Gerald R. Cragg, *The Church and the Age of Reason 1648-1789,* (Harmondsworth: Penguin, 1972), p. 50.
[4] Tim Harris, Paul Seaward, and Mark Goldie, *The Politics of Religion in Restoration England,* (Oxford: Blackwell, 1990), p. 15.

and execution of Charles I in 1649 by the Commonwealth was a recent memory.

Europe had been divided by the Thirty Years' War between Roman Catholics and Protestants from 1618 to 1648, and this also created a desire for settled political and religious security. The desire for such security was also seen in the continued opposition in England to Roman Catholic religion and politics, culminating in the Glorious Revolution of 1689, when the Roman Catholic King James II was removed and replaced by William and Mary. In general, Tories stood for Anglican exclusivism, while Whigs were more tolerant of dissent.[5]

3.2   Rival Reformations

Puritanism was also seen as inherently factious or fissiparous, liable to break up into different groups, and unable to agree and act together. In the words of John Spurr, 'English Revolution had splintered "the puritans" into Presbyterians, Independents, Baptists, Fifth-Monarchy Men, Quakers, Ranters, Muggletonians, Familists, and many more competing sects'.[6] To this list we must add Episcopalian Puritans, Reformed in theology, who worked to reform the Church of England, and who were committed to or content with Bishops, even if they supported the 'reduced episcopacy' suggested by Archbishop Ussher.[7] Of course Biblically committed Puritans, such as Anglicans, Presbyterians, Independents and Baptists were theologically remote from Quakers and others who trusted personal inspiration instead of the

---

[5]   Harris, et al., *Politics*, pp. 10,11.
[6]   John Spurr, 'Puritanism to Dissent', pp. 234-265.
[7]   Wallace Benn, 'Ussher on Bishops: A Reforming ecclesiology', in Lee Gatiss, [ed.], *Preachers, Pastors, Ambassadors: Puritan Wisdom for Today's Church, St Antholin's Lectures, Volume II, 2001-2010* (London: The Latimer Trust, 2011), pp. 97-122.

Bible.[8] However, public perception lumped all non-Anglicans together as Puritans, and then as nonconformists. It was understood that Puritanism was unstable, which was both politically alarming and religiously confusing.

Furthermore, some Puritans continued to pursue subversive political agendas, even during the Commonwealth. The Levellers were suppressed in 1649, the Ranters in 1651, the Diggers in 1650, and the Fifth Monarchists revolted unsuccessfully in 1657 and 1661. And the Quakers continued their revolutionary refusal to submit to civil authority.[9]

The main political conflict within the Commonwealth was between the Independents and the Presbyterians. Cromwell's aim was expressed in words of Richard Bosher:

> To make the Establishment the instrument for enforcing an almost unlimited tolerance of opinion, and for uniting warring groups in a common zeal for godliness was Cromwell's ideal... Hence he could regard with equanimity the crazy patch-work of the Commonwealth Church at the parish level – a spectacle that to Anglican and Presbyterian alike seemed an intolerable nightmare.[10]

All were to be included, except Popery, Prelacy, and antinomian Protestants.[11]

The Independents believed in the autonomy of the local congregation, while the Presbyterians believed in the structure of a national church, which is why they were more amenable to the restoration of the monarchy, and hoped for a reformed Church of

---

[8]   Peter Adam, 'Word and Spirit: the Puritan-Quaker Debate', in Lee Gatiss, [ed.], *Preachers, Pastors, Ambassadors, The St Antholin's Lectures, Volume II, 2001-2010,* (London: The Latimer Trust, 2011), pp. 49-96.

[9]   Christopher Hill, *A Turbulent, Seditious and Factious People: John Bunyan and his Church,* (Oxford: Oxford University Press, 1989), pp. 114,115.

[10] Bosher, *Restoration Settlement,* pp. 316,317.

[11] E.J. Poole-Connor, *Evangelicalism in England,* (Worthing: Walter, 1965), p. 106.

England in which they would feel at home.[12] This perception of controversy was also reflected in a cultural suspicion of Puritans. In the words of one contemporary:

> The Bible in English under every weaver's and chambermaid's arm hath done us royalists much harm...For controversy is a civil war with the pen which pulls out the sword soon afterwards.[13]

John Bunyan said that the Baptists were regarded as 'a turbulent, seditious and factious people',[14] and that was a common perception of all Puritans and all nonconformists. There was also a fear of antinomianism, of freedom from moral restraint, which was associated with the gospel of God's free grace associated with the Puritans.

From a different perspective, the Puritans themselves recognized that their unhappy divisions as a source of religious and political weakness. Richard Baxter commented, 'the sin of separating principles...cast the greatest dishonor on Religion that ever was done in England'.[15]

And how bewildering that those committed to the authority of the Bible, as were the Anglican, Presbyterian, Independent and Baptist Puritans, could disagree so deeply about its interpretation. As Christopher Hill observed, 'Popular diffusion and discussion of the Bible led, ironically, to a lessening of its authority.'[16] In the

---

[12] The theology and church structure the Independents is found in Savoy Platform of 1658, that of the Presbyterians in The Form of Presbyteral Church Government of 1645, and the Cambridge Platform, of 1648. See Iain Murray, [ed.], *The Reformation of the Church: A Collection of Reformed and Puritan Documents on Church Issues*, (Edinburgh: Banner of Truth, 1965), pp. 276-284, 207-233, 234-275.

[13] The Duke of Newcastle to Charles II, as quoted in Hill, *Turbulent*, p. 125.

[14] From John Bunyan, 'I will pray with the Spirit', as quoted in Hill, *Turbulent*, p. 111.

[15] Cliffe, *Puritans in Conflict*, p. 192.

[16] Christopher Hill, *The English Bible and the Seventeenth Century Revolution*, (London: Penguin, 1993), p. 432.

Church of England under the Commonwealth, the Prayer Book had been abandoned, and the *Westminster Directory of Public Worship* of 1645 was owned by less than a quarter of parishes, and in many churches only 'believers' were admitted to membership.[17] The different groups of Puritans wanted liberty for themselves, but not for others. As Cromwell complained, 'every sect says, oh, give me liberty. But give it him, and to his power he will not yield it to anybody else'.[18] Christopher Hill wrote, 'Calvinism disintegrated in the Revolution it had done so much to make possible.'[19]

No wonder John Whitlock, in his farewell sermon, urged his congregation to repent: 'Also, to repent of those sins, which have provoked, and may further provoke God to come among us as a thief, to take away many of His ministers from among us.'[20]

3.3   The failure of a cultural revolution

The Puritans had attempted a cultural revolution, and it had failed. The 'Rule of the Saints' had attempted to impose sanctity on the nation, in religious and daily life. The 1645 Directory for Public Worship formalized changes to the Christian Calendar, dropping holy days, including Christmas Day, and replacing them with secular monthly holidays, and monthly days of prayer and fasting. The Churching of Women was abandoned,[21] and marriages and funerals secularized. Activities like drinking, gaming, dancing, and the theatre were reduced.[22] The Commonwealth could have been

---

[17]   Spurr, *Post-Reformation*, pp. 134, 135.

[18]   Spurr, *Post-Reformation*, p. 136.

[19]   Christopher Hill, *Puritanism and Revolution: Studies in Interpretation of the English Revolution of the 17th Century*, (London: Secker and Warburg, 1958), p. 238

[20]   Murray, *Sermons*, p. 177.

[21]   The Churching of Women was a service for women after childbirth. In 1662 it is called, 'The Thanksgiving of Women after Childbirth'.

[22]   Christoper Durston, 'Puritan Rule and the Failure of Cultural Revolution,' in Christopher Durston and Jacqueline Eales, [eds.], *The Culture of English Puritanism 1560-1700*, (Houndmills: Macmillan, 1996), pp. 210-233.

accused of 'provoking' people unnecessarily, and certainly there was strong reaction against these changes and restrictions.[23] Even in highly Puritan Dorchester the tolling of the church bell at funerals continued contrary to regulation.[24] David Underdown has written of the obstinate tenacity of popular cultural traditions, and of the 'chorus of mocking laughter' that greeted attempts to change them.[25] In the words of Richard Baxter,

> Custom is the thing that sways much with the multitude; and they that first break a destructive custom must bear the brunt of their [the people's] indignation.[26]

It was characteristic of Puritans to hasten reform: perhaps they hastened it too quickly, and by doing so provoked opposition. In John Oldfield's farewell sermon, he described how he and his fellow Puritans were regarded by people as,

> busy, censorious, pragmatical fellows, making divisions and separations among our people, taking upon us power to suspend you from the Lord's Table, admitting and excluding whom we pleased, exercising a power more arbitrary than ever the Bishops did.[27]

3.4 Puritan scholastic preaching

The mood of the times was also opposed to any form of scholasticism, Protestant or Roman Catholic.[28] Detailed academic and intellectual ways of doing theology were suspect, including scholastic Reformed Theology. Protestants had been irretrievably

---

[23] Durston, 'Rule', p. 220.
[24] David Underdown, *Fire from Heaven: The Life in an English Town in the Seventeenth Century*, (London: Pimlico, 2003), p. 218.
[25] Underdown, *Fire*, pp. 264-5.
[26] As quoted in Durston, 'Rule', p. 233
[27] As quoted in Murray, *Sermons*, 163.
[28] See Basil Willey, *The Seventeenth-Century Background*, (Harmondsworth: Penguin, 1962), pp. 9ff and pp. 155ff.

divided in England and Europe over theological issues, with drastic political consequences. Puritans were 'precisionists', because, in the words of Richard Rodgers, 'I serve a precise God'.[29] A more common-sense approach was now called for, and more emphasis on the plain common truths of Christianity that would unite all Christians, and on plain moral Christian duties. Puritan precision about theology, about church practice, and about morality[30] was increasingly unconvincing and unpopular, and seen as practically and politically divisive.

Puritan preaching tended to be scholastic, that is, detailed, analytic, and comprehensive. Puritan preaching was similar to the Medieval scholastic sermon,[31] with a short text of Scripture dissected and analysed, and then an extensive and intensive application of the text, with many points of 'Doctrine' (the theological significance of the text) and 'Use' (application of the text).[32] Each point then had many sub-points. It was an attempt to communicate a vast mass of material without confusion, but it could have been overwhelming. Furthermore, both Doctrine and Use were so comprehensive that the Bible text was easily obscured by the volume of material being expounded. What may have been appropriate in a university, monastery, or court was now being used in local churches, with many uneducated and illiterate hearers. And it was accepted practice to preach a series of sermons

---

[29] Richard Rodgers, as quoted in Leland Ryken, *Worldly Saints: The Puritans As They Really Were*, (Grand Rapids: Academie, 1990), p. 5.

[30] Detailed Puritan morality is seen for example in Richard Baxter's *A Christian Directory, Baxter's Practical Works Vol. I*, Reprint, (Ligonier: Soli Deo Gloria, 1990). See also David Field, '"Decalogue" Dod and his Seventeenth Century Bestseller: a 400th Anniversary Appreciation', in Gatiss, Lee, [ed.], *Preachers, Pastors and Ambassadors, The St Antholin's Lectures, Volume II, 2001-2010*, (London: The Latimer Trust, 2011), pp. 149-204.

[31] Charles Smyth, *The Art of Preaching: 747-1939* (London: SPCK, 1940), pp. 19-35, and H. Leith Spencer, *English Preaching in the Late Middle Ages*, (Oxford: Clarendon, 1993), pp. 228-268.

[32] See William Perkins, *The Art of Prophesying, The Calling of the Ministry*, (Edinburgh: Banner of Truth, 1996), pp. 48-68.

on the Westminster Catechism.[33] While these sermons began with a short text of Scripture, the real text of the sermon was the quotation from the Catechism that followed it. This was not inappropriate, but again the scripture itself was overwhelmed by the theology and ethics. As Hughes Oliphant Old wrote, 'English Puritanism is an expression of Protestant scholasticism.'[34]

Of course its motivation was excellent. The combination of precision in exegesis, doctrine and application led to long sermons, with much detailed argument and evidence. In the words of Gerald Cragg, 'exactness in exegesis and the use of formal logical distinctions were thus among the indispensable weapons in the armoury of the Puritan preacher.'[35] Hour-long sermons were the order of the day, for Puritans and others alike.[36] And such preaching was popular, as is evident in lay support for more preaching through the appointment of Lecturers in churches.[37] Such preaching was demanding for the preacher because it was so precise and comprehensive. For the listeners it demanded great energy to listen attentively and to be challenged educationally for such long periods. There were obviously some people who enjoyed the intellectual stimulation of long sermons; and it may be that it was published sermons that followed this style most strongly. It was attractive to gathered congregations, but less popular as a compulsory diet. It may well be that some Puritan preachers in England did adopt a simpler style, especially in rural contexts.[38]

It was a pity that the Puritans largely adopted this style of

---

[33] Thomas Watson, *A Body of Divinity,* (London: Banner of Truth, 1958).

[34] Hughes Oliphant Old, *The Reading and Preaching of the Scriptures in the Worship of the Christian Church, Volume 4, The Age of the Reformation,* (Grand Rapids and Cambridge: Eerdmans, 2002), p. 326.

[35] Cragg, *Puritanism, Persecution,* pp. 208, 229.

[36] Cragg, *Puritanism, Persecution,* pp. 201-219.

[37] Paul S. Seaver, *The Puritan Lectureships,* (Stanford: Stanford University Press, 1970).

[38] Arnold Hunt, *The Art of Hearing: English preachers and their Audiences, 1590-1640,* University of Cambridge PhD Thesis, 1998, pp. 158-202.

preaching, because John Calvin had created a new style of expository preaching that was simpler, more accessible, less detailed, more straight-forward, easier to follow, and shorter![39] Calvin's sermons were translated into English, and were widely read in England in the 16th Century.[40] Calvin's style of expository preaching reflected that of the Early Church, notably in the preaching of Augustine and John Chrysostom. This preaching had been know in England, and was favoured by Wycliffe.[41] It was retained in the Restoration Reformed episcopal Church of Scotland from 1662 to 1689, in the ministry of Archbishop Leighton and Henry Scougal, who '...revived the practice of commenting on a whole chapter or large portion of Scripture, believing it to be the most edifying style of preaching'.[42] But by the 17th Century, many English Puritans had reverted to the more complicated scholastic medieval style. The Puritan style was both precise and comprehensive in its use of the Bible, its theology, and its application, and this was the style of preaching taken to America by the Puritans, and followed by such leaders as Jonathan Edwards. Edwards wisely adopted a less complicated style in his sermons to the American Indians.[43] But the usual pattern of Puritan preaching set too high a standard for ordinary people, and became increasingly culturally inappropriate and unacceptable. It was scholasticism misapplied. Joseph Carryl was pastorally motivated

---

[39] See my '"Preaching of a Lively Kind": Calvin's engaged expository preaching', in *Engaging with Calvin. Aspects of the Reformer's legacy for today'*, Mark D. Thompson [ed.], Apollos, Nottingham, 2009; and also 'Calvin's Preaching and Homiletic: Nine Engagements', Parts 1 and 2, *Churchman*, Vol. 124, Nos. 3 and 4, 2010. See also, Old, *Reading, Preaching*, pp. 90-133.

[40] See T.H.L. Parker, *The Oracles of God: an Introduction to the Preaching of John Calvin* (London and Redhill: Lutterworth, 1947), and T.H.L. Parker, *Calvin's Preaching*, (Edinburgh: T&T Clark, 1992).

[41] Spencer, *English Preaching*, pp. 228-268.

[42] Scougal, Henry, *The Works of Henry Scougal 1650-1678*, (Morgan: Soli Deo Gloria, 2002), p. xii.

[43] W.H. Kimnach, K.P. Minkeema, and D.A. Sweeny, [eds.], *The Sermons of Jonathan Edwards: A Reader*, (New Haven and London: Yale University Press, 1999), p. xxxv.

to preach on the book of Job, because he thought it was an appropriate book for a suffering church. But he was perhaps pastorally unwise to continue his series on the book of Job for 29 years.[44] Such preaching lost the momentum of the book, and worked too hard to find relevance in every word of the book.[45]

We also need to accept that sermons remained popular from the 16th to the 19th Century. So Jane Austen's Mary Bennett was addicted to Fordyce's sermons, and Charles Spurgeon's sermons were famously popular in the 19th Century.

However the intensely detailed and comprehensive approach to preaching scholastic preaching reflected the precision and comprehensiveness of the Puritan world-view and approach to every part of life and ministry. It became increasingly out of fashion during the 17th Century. George Herbert had earlier urged a simpler method:

> The Countrey Parson preacheth constantly, the pulpit is his joy and his throne: ... The Parsons Method in handling of a text consists of two parts; first, a plain and evident declaration of the meaning of the text; and secondly, some choyce Observations drawn out of the whole text, as it lyes entire, and unbroken in the Scripture it self...Whereas the other way of crumbling a text into small parts...hath neither in it sweetnesse, nor gravity, nor variety, since the words apart are not Scripture, but a dictionary...[46]

The preaching that eventually shook the nation was that of the

---

[44] William S. Barker, *Puritan Profiles,* (Fearn: Mentor, 1996), pp. 127-130

[45] For more on Puritan preaching, see Chad B. Van Dixhorn, 'A Puritan Theology of Preaching', in Lee Gatiss, [ed.], *Preachers, Pastors and Ambassadors, The St Antholin's Lectures, Volume II, 2001-2010,* (London: The Latimer Trust, 2011), pp. 206-259.

[46] George Herbert, *The Priest to the Temple, or, The Country Parson,* in *The Works of George Herbert,* F.E. Hutchinson [ed.], (Oxford: Clarendon Press, 1941), p. 235.

Evangelical Revival, which began in the 1730s. A good example of that style was George Whitefield, whose preaching was Biblical, passionate, direct, plain, easy to follow, and powerful.[47]

3.5 Class divisions?

Christopher Hill suggests that anti-Puritan sentiment, the Act of Uniformity of 1662, and the persecution that followed were also motivated by snobbery. Nonconformists such as Baptists were regarded as the 'poorer and meaner people', while the Restoration brought back government by the nobility and principal gentry.[48] The Restoration was also followed by enclosure of common land and the oppression of the poor and the lower classes.[49] Archbishop Bancroft had said many years earlier, attacking Presbyterian Puritans, that among them the kingdom of Christ is, 'nowhere acknowledged or to be found but where half a dozen artisans, shoemakers and tinkers...do rule the whole parish.'[50] On the other hand, as Harold Wood points out, of those who did not conform, 1285 were university graduates.[51]

Even though there were many Puritans who were gentry, it had still been a shock for England to find the lower classes demanding to be heard in religion and in politics.

---

[47] George Whitefield, *The Sermons of George Whitefield*, Parts 1 and 2, Lee Gatiss [ed.], (Watford: Church Society, 2010), and Arnold Dallimore, *George Whitefield: the life and times of the great evangelist of the 18th century revival*, Vol. 1, (London: Banner of Truth, 1970), pp. 103-130, 249-270. And for a broader perspective, see Ashley Null, 'Thomas Cranmer and Tudor Evangelicalism', in Michael A.G. Haykin and Kenneth J. Stewart, [eds.], *The Emergence of Evangelicalism: Exploring Historical Continuities*, (Nottingham: Apollos, 2008), pp. 221-251.
[48] Hill, *Turbulent*, pp. 114,112, and see also pp. 125-130.
[49] Hill, *Turbulent*, pp. 111-114.
[50] As quoted in Hill, *Turbulent*, 136
[51] Wood, *Church unity*, p. 231.

3.6   The weakening of Reformed churches and theology

We should recognize that Reformed churches and theology had suffered significant set-backs and reduction across Europe. There had been persecution and extermination in France, culminating in the St Bartholomew Day massacre of 1572, with the consequent departure of many of the Huguenots. The Reformed Church in Lithuania and Poland had fallen into Arianism and Unitarianism by 1600. The collapse of the Palatinate in 1620 marked a significant decline in Reformed power in Europe. According to Augustus Toplady, the ministers of Geneva had become Arminian by 1690.[52] Jean Jacques Rousseau lived in Geneva, and the following words about the ministers of Geneva in the 18th Century are attributed to him: 'We neither know what they believe or what they do not believe. We do not even know what they pretend to believe.'[53]

G.R. Cragg wrote of Calvinism in England: 'At the beginning of the century, it had dominated the religious life of England: by the end its power had been completely overthrown.'[54] This is an overstatement, as we will see, but points to a significant weakening of Reformed theology and practice.

Internationally, Reformed theology had been weakened by the Arminian controversy, which began as a reformation of Calvinism, but soon produced an alternative theological system. Arminianism had entered the Church of England in the 1600s, and within Baptist churches there were two theological systems, Calvinist and Arminian. Reformed theology had also been weakened by an internal debate about the extent of Christ's atonement, on whether he died for the elect or for the world. This

---

[52]   Augustus Toplady, 'Historical Proof of the Doctrinal Calvinisim of the Church of England', *The Complete Works of Augustus Toplady*, (Harrisonburg: Sprinkle, 1987 {1794}), pp. 64-306, and the reference to Geneva is on p. 64.

[53]   I have not been able to find these words in Rousseau's writings. They are quoted in the Calvin Museum in Geneva.

[54]   Cragg, *Puritanism, Reason*, p. 13, and see pp.13-36.

was the Amyraldian controversy, which divided Reformed theology from the 1620s.[55]

In England Reformed thought and practice had been adjusted and corrected by many within the Church of England and beyond it. Its sources lay in the Swiss Reformation before Calvin; in Calvin himself with his *Institutes,* Commentaries, and sermons; the influence of Geneva itself as a home for English refugees; in Heinrich Bullinger, and Theodore Beza whose writings and sermons were very influential;[56] and in Martin Bucer and Peter Martyr Vermigli, both of whom had taught in England, and significantly influenced the 1552 *Book of Common Prayer.*[57] This Reformed theology and practice was worked out in the context of other influences, including the theology of Martin Luther, and groups of Lollards.[58] The churches of Edward VI, Elizabeth and James were generally Reformed in theology and practice.

However as early as the 1620s, some of the Calvinist ministers had become Cambridge Platonists. This movement rejected the dogmatic strictness of Calvinism, and placed more trust in reason, that 'candle of the Lord' which is in everyone. They linked reason and morality, and wanted to learn how to live in God's world in God's way.[59] According to John Passmore, 'Cambridge Platonism was primarily a rejection of Calvinism'.[60]

---

[55] Lee Gatiss, *For Us and For Our Salvation: 'Limited Atonement' in Bible, Doctrine, History, Theology and Ministry,* (London: The Latimer Trust, 2012).

[56] On Beza see Marvin W. Anderson, *Evangelical Foundations: Religion in England, 1378-1683,* (New York: Lang, 1987), pp. 171-188.

[57] On Bucer see Martin Greschat, *Martin Bucer: A Reformer and his times,* (Louisville: Westminster John Knox, 2004), pp. 227-254; and on Peter Martyr, Joseph C. McClelland, *The Visible Words of God: An Exposition of the Sacramental theology of Peter Martyr Vermigli, 1500-1562,* (Edinburgh: Oliver and Boyd, 1957).

[58] On Luther see Dickens, *English Reformation,* pp. 59-74, and on the Lollards, see Dickens, *English Reformation,* pp. 22-37, and Anderson, *Foundations,* pp. 368-370.

[59] Willey, *Background,* pp. 123ff, Field, *Howe,* pp. 112-120.

[60] As quoted in Field, *Howe,* p. 112.

They were followed by the Latitudinarians, who placed even more trust in reason, and whose theological method was to work out a reasonable theology, and then find support for it from the Bible.[61] Arminianism also arrived in the Church of England in the 1600s, and was associated with more high-church practices under Archbishop Laud.

Reformed Calvinist theology was also weakened by the rise of the Quakers in the 1630s. The Quakers dispensed with the Bible and tradition, and trusted the Spirit within, often experienced with deep emotion, and with physical expressions of emotion. Many of the early Quakers were children of Puritan parents.[62] Both Cambridge Platonists and Quakers trusted an internal authority, reason for the Cambridge Platonists, and emotion for the Quakers.

Deism was also gaining ground. Its first exponent was Lord Herbert of Cherbury in the 1630s and 40s. It was based on a thorough commitment to reason, it was opposed to superstitious supernaturalism, and restricted God to his role in creation. Its later exponent was John Toland, who published *Christianity not Mysterious* in 1696. Even within the two powerful movements of the Commonwealth, Independency and Presbyterianism, true godliness was in decline. Lucy Hutchinson commented on religious life under the Commonwealth, 'True religion was now almost lost, even among the religious party, and Hipocrisie became an epidemicall disease'.[63]

Among the nonconformists, some Independents and Baptists were Calvinist in some respects, even if they did not follow Calvin's views on church polity and or infant baptism, and others were not. The Presbyterians after 1662 divided on the issue of Calvinism, and a new 'moderate Calvinism' was preached, as we

---

[61] Martin I.J., Griffin, Jr., *Latitudinarians of the Seventeenth Century Church of England*, (Leiden: Brill, 1992).

[62] Adam, 'Word and Spirit', pp. 49-96.

[63] In Cliffe, *Puritans in Conflict*, p. 192.

have already seen.[64] The prominent nonconformist Richard Baxter came to a modified Calvinist view on justification which was remarkably similar to that of earlier non-Reformed Anglicans.[65] On the Anglican side, Bishop Bull published his *Harmonia Apostolica* in 1670, in which he harmonized Paul and James on justification by interpreting Paul in the light of James.[66]

There was a move towards Arianism and Unitarianism both within the Church of England, and within Nonconformity. Dr Samuel Clarke, Anglican Unitarian, published an annotated *Book of Common Prayer*, a radical revision of the liturgy, which was used extensively by Anglican and Nonconformists, as 'the Arian blight' spread rapidly through England.[67] Samuel Clarke espoused Arianism and Unitarianism in his *Scripture Doctrine of the Trinity* of 1712.[68] This was part of wider move to Unitarianism.[69] All this in turn led to a strong defence of Christian orthodoxy in the early 18th Century by Anglicans. These included Joseph Butler's defence of the doctrine of God in his *Analogy of Religion* of 1736, and Daniel Waterland's defence of Trinitarian theology in his *Vindication of Christ's Divinity* of 1719, his *Second Vindication of Christ's Divinity* of 1723, and his *Importance of the Doctrine of the Holy Trinity asserted* of 1734.[70] John Owen defended Trinitarian

[64] Field, *Howe,* pp. 18-33.

[65] C. Fitzsimmons Allison, *The Rise of Moralism: the Proclamation of The Gospel from Hooker to Baxter,* (Wilton: Morehouse Barlow, 1966), pp. 154-164.

[66] Allison, *Moralism,* pp. 118-137.

[67] Charles Linnell, *Some East Anglian Clergy,* (London: The Faith Press, 1961) pp. 80-85.

[68] See J.P. Ferguson, *Dr Samuel Clarke: An Eighteenth Century Heretic,* (Kineton: Roundwood, 1976).

[69] John Redwood, *Reason, Ridicule and Religion: The Age of Enlightenment in England 1660-1750,* (London: Thames and Hudson, 1976), pp. 156-173.

[70] J.H. Overton and F. Relton, *The English Church from the Accession of George I to the end of the Eighteenth Century [1714-1800],* (London: Macmillan, 1906), pp. 4,5.

orthodoxy in his writing from the 1650s,[71] but this kind of defence was provided by Anglicans after 1662. Within and beyond the Church of England orthodox faith was under attack, and was defended. Atheism was now publicly espoused, and both reason and ridicule were used to attack Christianity and the church.[72] In the words of Archbishop Secker, 'Christianity is now railed at and ridiculed with very little reserve, and its teachers without any at all.'[73]

Baptists were divided between Calvinists and Arminians, as we have seen. Some Calvinist Baptists became Hyper-Calvinist, after the publication of Tobias Crisp's writings in 1689.[74] This view was later expressed in the famous rebuff to William Carey's ideas of evangelizing India, 'Young man, sit down; when God pleases to convert the heathen, he will do it without your aid or mine.'[75] Debate about Crisp's ideas also caused a division between Presbyterians and Hyper-Calvinist Independents in 1694.

Even in Puritan New England, there were growing signs of declension. Jonathan Edwards warned in 1739 that Quakers, Socinians, Arminians, Arians and Deists were flourishing, and described this as an unprecedented apostasy on the part of those who had been nurtured in Reformed Theology.[76]

Even the Reformed theology of the *Thirty-Nine Articles* for the Anglicans and the *Westminster Confession* for the

---

[71] See Carl R. Trueman, *The Claims of Truth: John Owen's Trinitarian Theology*, (Carlisle: Paternoster, 1998), pp. 102-198.

[72] Redwood, *Reason, Ridicule*, pp. 29-92, and 174-213.

[73] Cragg, *Church, Reason*, p. 127.

[74] Peter Toon, *The Emergence of Hyper-Calvinism in English Nonconformity 1689-1765*, (London: Olive Tree, 1967); and T.E. Watson, 'Andrew Fuller's conflict with Hypercalvinism', pp. 271-282, in D. Martyn Lloyd-Jones [ed.], *Puritan Papers, Volume One, 1956-1959*, (Phillipsburg: P&R, 2001).

[75] F. Deaville Walker, *William Carey, missionary pioneer and statesman*, (London: SCM, 1926), p. 63. The words are attributed to J.R. Ryland. The quotation is disputed.

[76] George M. Marsden, *Jonathan Edwards: A Life*, (New Haven: Yale University Press, 2003), p. 199.

Presbyterians could not restrain the drift away from Reformed theology and practice.

The English Reformed consensus of the early 17th Century had eroded, and this had occurred independently of the events of 1662. Yet, as we will see, Reformed witness continued after 1662, both within the Church of England and among nonconformists. Indeed one of the bad effects of 1662 was the division it caused between Reformed Anglicans and Reformed nonconformists.

3.7 Frustration and impatience

How discouraging to see the work of reforming the church being set back decades. The 16th Century had seemed bright with the hope of reformation and renewal, and now so much had been lost. The reintroduction of traditional Anglicanism must have seemed like a large step backwards.

And while some of the rhetoric of the Church of England appeared to promise liberty, the practice was very different. For they could read these words in one of the Prefaces to the *Book of Common Prayer:*

> Christ's Gospel is not a Ceremonial Law, (as much of Moses' Law was,) but it is a Religion to serve God, not in bondage of the figure or shadow, but in the freedom of the Spirit; being content only with those Ceremonies which do Serve to a decent Order and godly Discipline, and such as be apt to stir up the dull mind of man to the remembrance of his duty to God, by some notable and special signification, whereby he might be edified.[77]

The Act of Uniformity felt like bondage, not liberty.

When is it right to leave a church and its ministry? Many years before 1662 Thomas Cartwright had answered those Puritans

---

[77] *The Book of Common Prayer,* 1662, Preface, 'Of Ceremonies'.

who claimed that the church was so corrupt that true believers should leave it. Peter Lake has summarised his arguments:

i.   The church must be mixed, as it is made up of people who are a mixture of grace and sin. The search for a pure church is doomed to failure.

ii. The church is like a disobedient wife: still a wife 'not having abandoned her husband by atheism nor by idolatry'.

iii. It is wrong to judge before the time. The time for the separation of sheep and goats is at the return of Christ, and not before.

iv. Christ did not separate himself from the church of his time, even though the people of God had allowed corruptions to enter into holy things, and despite the enmity of the leaders of God's people against him.

v.   Peter and the other apostles still treated the Jews as the people of God, despite their sins.

vi. The Church of England still retained the preaching of the Word, ministry and sacraments, and so continued to be the church of God.

vii. As in the church the godly were 'the leaven that leavened the whole lump,' so in the church's ministry it is the activity of Puritan ministers that helps the church remain the church of God.[78]

So why did so many leave? As we have seen, there were different reasons for different people. For some, it was the requirement to be ordained again. For others, it was the requirement to use the *Book of Common Prayer* exclusively. For others, it was the reintroduction of Diocesan Bishops. For others, it was the demands of a conformist church. For others, it was the removal of

---

[78] Peter Lake, *Moderate Puritans and the Elizabethan Church*, (Cambridge: Cambridge University Press, 1982), pp. 80-86.

the right of ministers to exercise pastoral discipline in their churches. For many, no doubt, it was a combination of these. Was it right to leave or to stay? It is not for us to say: each one of us is accountable to God, not to each other.[79]

Thomas Watson, in his farewell sermon, recognized that suffering is part of living as a believer:

> However, we must go to heaven through good report and bad report; and it is well if we can get to glory, though we pass through the pikes.[80]

3.8 Judgement for sin

One of the powerful Puritan themes is the present judgements of God. And one reason they gave for the trials of 1662 was that God was judging them. As we have seen, John Whitlock warned his people in his farewell sermon,

> Also, to repent of those sins, which have provoked, and may further provoke God to come among us as a thief, to take away many of His ministers from among us.[81]

And in his final sermon, John Collins confessed: 'Our zeal has been so hot against one another for mere externals and so cold when we are likely to lose the substance.'[82]

Edward Calamy was offered the bishopric of Lichfield and Coventry if he conformed, but he declined it, and resigned. In this recognition of God's judgement on the sins of the godly, he quoted John Bradford:

> Lord, it was my unthankfulness for the gospel, that brought in popery in Queen Mary's days; and my unfruitfulness

---

[79] Romans 14:12.
[80] Watson, *Divinity*, p. vii.
[81] Murray, *Sermons*, p. 177.
[82] Murray, *Sermons*, p. 59.

under the gospel that was the cause of the untimely death of King Edward the Sixth.[83]

And he acknowledged, 'There is a strange kind of indifference and lukewarmness upon most people's spirits.'[84] The famous London preacher Thomas Brooks, in his final sermon, said: 'God has made His wrath to smoke against us for the divisions and heart-burnings that have been among us.'[85]

The active Puritan conscience was quick to acknowledge sin, and to recognize the chastening hand of God. Yet God's grace was still to be expected, even in a time of judgment. So John Collins also trusted that God in his mercy would still use his life under gospel trials, even though he would be unable to preach from his church pulpit:

> You mistake if you think that we have done preaching; no, we are only called to preach to you out of the pulpit of the cross...And why may it not be hoped that our preaching out of that pulpit may be more effectual than out of this? ...If my sufferings attain their end, which is your consolation and salvation, I shall through grace bless God, in making use of me to that purpose. He can make our silence speak louder and more effectually than all our sermons have done.[86]

[83]   Murray, *Sermons*, p. 26.
[84]   Murray, *Sermons*, p. 28.
[85]   Murray, *Sermons*, p. 46.
[86]   Murray, *Sermons*, pp. 171,172.

4. What did it mean, and what was the result?

4.1 For the Church of England

4.1.1 A Reformed Church?

The loss of 1760 ministers weakened the Church of England. Did it mean that the Church of England was no longer Reformed, and that Puritans had no place in it?

We should not think that this meant the removal of Reformed or Puritan ministry from the Church. As I.M. Green points out, more clergy who had been active in the Commonwealth continued their ministries than resigned them.[1] Moderate Puritans remained within the Church of England. They included significant leaders like Bishop Reynolds of Norwich. Stephen Hampton has identified the significant presence of Reformed Anglicans in the Restoration Church of England, including 12 Bishops, 6 Deans, and a group of able theologians in Oxford.[2] He points to a greater interest in church buildings in this Restoration Reformed church, though Edmund Grindal, Bishop of London and then Archbishop of Canterbury at the time of Elizabeth had worked hard to rebuild St Paul's Cathedral London.[3] Even leaders like Bishop Henry Compton, Bishop of London from 1675, though not identified with Reformed or Puritan ideas, was firmly Protestant, had a sound Biblical faith, recognized the authority of the Bible, and was opposed to Arminianism.[4] Reformed Anglican theologians such as

---

[1] Green, *Re-Establishment*, p. 177. See also John Spurr, *English Puritanism, 1603-1689*, (Houndmills: Macmillan, 1998), p. 131.

[2] Stephen Hampton, *Anti-Arminians: The Anglican Reformed Tradition from Charles II to George I*, (Oxford, Oxford University Press, 2008), pp. 1-38.

[3] Patrick Collinson, *Archbishop Grindal, 1519-1583: The Struggle for a Reformed Church*, (London: Jonathan Cape, 1979), pp. 153-161.

[4] Edward Carpenter, *The Protestant Bishop: Being the Life of Henry Compton, 1632-1713, Bishop of London*, (London: Longmans, 1956), and Hampton, *Anti-Arminians*, p. 14.

Bishop John Pearson wrote his exposition of the Creed which was 'the most highly esteemed book of dogmatic theology of later stuart period', and Robert South ably defended the doctrine of the Trinity in the 1690s.[5] And some lay Anglicans still objected to the more high-church practices introduced by Archbishop Laud. So Andrew Marvell, poet and MP, wrote in 1672 of the Laudian innovations of the 1630s:

> There was a second service, the table set altar-wise, and to be called the altar; candles, crucifixes, paintings, images, copes, bowing to the east bowing to the altar, and so many several cringes and genuflexions that a man unpracticed stood in need to entertain both a dancing-master and a remembrancer.[6]

Lee Gatiss has written of the Reformed Anglican identity of St Helen's Bishopsgate, served by the Dr Thomas Horton, who conformed in 1662.[7] An ordinary parish minister like William Burkitt, Vicar of Dedham, wrote his widely used *Expository Notes on the New Testament*, published in 1700-1704.[8] This book inspired the nonconformist Presbyterian Matthew Henry to write his famous *Commentary on the Whole Bible*, between 1704 and 1714. This in turn later inspired the Anglican Thomas Haweis of the Evangelical Revival to publish his *The Evangelical Expositor, or*

---

[5] Hampton, *Anti-Arminians*, pp. 34, 129-161. See John Pearson, *An Exposition of the Creed*, W.S. Dobson [ed.], (London: Scott, Webster and Geary, 1842).

[6] Andrew Marvell, *Selected Poetry and Prose*, Robert Wilcher [ed.], (London: Methuen, 1986), p. 147. The quotation is from 'The Rehearsal Transpos'd'.

[7] Lee Gatiss, *The Tragedy of 1662: The Ejection and Persecution of the Puritans*, Latimer Studies 66, (London: The Latimer Trust, 2007), pp. 45,46; and Lee Gatiss, *The True Profession of the Gospel: Augustus Toplady and reclaiming our Reformed foundations*, (London: Latimer Trust, 2010), pp. 35-39.

[8] William Burkitt, *Expository Notes, with Practical Observations on the New Testament of our Lord and Saviour Jesus Christ*, (Liverpool: Caxton, nd).

Commentary on the Whole Bible... in 1766.[9] Here was a shared inheritance of Reformed Biblical exposition shared between the Church of England and nonconformists, of benefit to lay people and ministers alike. And from 1662-1689, there were Reformed Episcopalians north of the border in the Church of Scotland, including those with a significant ministry of Bible exposition and devotional writing, such as Archbishop Leighton and Henry Scougal.[10]

This is an important issue when evaluating the significance of the resignations and ejections of ministers in 1660-1662. It is commonly held that those who left were all the Puritans, or all the Reformed ministers and people, and that the Church of England was now free of Puritan or Reformed ministers or people. That is not true, as we have seen. Furthermore, not all nonconformists were Puritan or Reformed. So the simple and common distinction made between conforming non-Reformed Anglicans and nonconformist Reformed Puritans will not work.[11] Furthermore, a number of clergy who conformed were not diligent in the practice of conformity. Certainly an early report to Sheldon, by then Archbishop of Canterbury, provided evidence of significant continuity of nonconforming practice in the Church of England.[12] Ronald Hutton observed that 'the Church of Charles II had as much casual nonconformity as that of James I', not least because Latitudinarian bishops, who were committed to reasonable basic faith in God and in moral decency, were lax in enforcing

9   Thomas Haweis, *The Evangelical Expositor, or Commentary on the Whole Bible...* (Glasgow: Somerville, Fullarton Blackie, 1822), and see Arthur Skevington Wood, *Thomas Haweis 1734-1820*, (London: SPCK, 1957), pp. 115-126.
10 See Robert Leighton, 'A Practical Commentary on the First Epistle General of St Peter', *The Whole Works of Robert Leighton*, Vol. I, J.N. Pearson [ed.], (London: James Duncan, 1835), pp. 109-609; and Scougal, *Works*.
11 The issue is further complicated by the use of 'Puritan' to mean all nonconformists including Quakers, as in Cragg, *Puritanism, Persecution*.
12 Green, *Re-Establishment*, p. 170

conformity.[13] In the words of C.W. Dugmore, 'the Latitudinarians agreed with the Deists...that the essentials of religion are few and simple, so that there is no need to insist on High Church or Puritan shibboleths'.[14] And some Puritan patrons of parishes were diligent in finding Puritan conforming clergy.[15]

Richard Baxter wrote of two brands of Anglicans in the Restoration Church:

> some lately sprung up, that follow Archbishop Laud...And these seemed uppermost in 1660, 1661...The other Episcopal conformists are they that follow the REFORMERS, and hold the doctrine of Scripture as only sufficient for salvation, and as explicatory of it, the Thirty-nine Articles...[16]

Two groups of people prefer the theory that Puritans cannot be Anglicans, nor can Anglicans be Puritans.[17] Some Nonconformists may take this view because they want to emphasise the gulf between Anglicanism and Puritanism, to show that true Puritanism is found outside Anglicanism. Some Anglican writers take this view because they want to claim that Puritanism has no place in mainstream Anglicanism. However Patrick Collinson has shown that Puritanism was part of Anglicanism: 'our modern conception [that] Anglicanism commonly excludes puritanism is...a distortion of part of our religious history'.[18] A.G. Dickens claimed that:

---

[13] Ronald Hutton, *The Restoration: A Political and Religious History of England and Wales 1658-1667*, (Oxford: Clarendon, 1985), p. 288.

[14] C.W. Dugmore, *Eucharistic Doctrine in England from Hooker to Waterland*, (London: SPCK, 1942), p. 135.

[15] Green, *Re-Establishment*, pp. 153,154.

[16] As quoted in Wood, *Church unity*, p. 241.

[17] I have also expressed these ideas in Peter Adam, 'A Church "Halfly Reformed": the Puritan Dilemma' republished in Lee Gatiss, [ed.], *Pilgrims, Warriors, and Servants, The St Antholin's Lectures, Volume 1, 1991-2000*, (London: The Latimer Trust, 2010), pp. 185-215.

[18] Patrick Collinson, *The Elizabethan Puritan Movement*, (London: Jonathan

Puritanism in our sense was never limited to Nonconformists; it was a powerful element in the origins of the Anglican Church and it was through that Church that it won its abiding role in the life and outlook of the nation.[19]

Robert Bosher has argued that the Settlement of 1662 was a repudiation of Reformed Anglicanism.

In the Elizabethan settlement the Reformation had been given a peculiarly English expression, and we may interpret the settlement of 1662 as an equally characteristic English version of the Counter-Reformation.[20]

The English Reformation was characteristically English, as the Reformations in other nations were characteristic of those nations. However Bosher gives no evidence to support his claim that the 1662 Settlement was a version of the Counter-Reformation. In fact the evidence in his book points the other way.

The revision of the *Book of Common Prayer* in 1662 had only minor changes in a more 'high-church' direction as he points out. These included the blessing the water in Baptism, standing for the gospel reading and Creed, and the provision for consecrating more bread and wine if required in Holy Communion. He omits the fact that the very Protestant Black Rubric at the end of the

---

Cape, 1967), p. 467.

[19] A.G. Dickens, *The English Reformation*, (London: Collins, 1967), p. 428. And see also: Mark Dever, *Richard Sibbes: Puritanism and Calvinism in Late Elizabethan and Early Stuart England*, (Macon: Mercer University Press, 2000); Kenneth Fincham, *Prelate as Pastor: the Episcopate of James I*, (Oxford: Oxford University Press, 1990); Kenneth Fincham, *The Early Stuart Church 1603-1642*, (Stanford: Stanford University Press, 1993); Lake, *Moderate Puritans*; N. Tyacke, *Aspects of English Protestantism, c.1530-1700*, (Manchester: Manchester University Press, 2001); and Tom Webster, *Godly Clergy in Early Stuart England: The Caroline Puritan Movement c1620-1643*, (Cambridge: Cambridge University Press, 1997).

[20] Bosher, *Restoration Settlement*, p. 282.

service for the Lord's Supper from 1552 but omitted in 1559 was reinserted in 1662. The 1662 Book is like the 1552 Book, not the 1549 Book: it uses 'table' rather than 'altar',[21] and makes no mention of the Lord's Supper as a sacrifice. The service was to taken from the North End of the table, not from the East-facing position used by the Roman Catholic Church and favoured by Archbishop Laud. And it was still permissible for the Holy Table to be in the body of the Church, rather than in a Laudian sanctuary, against the east wall of the building.

> The Table at the Communion time having a fair white linen cloth upon it, shall stand in the body of the Church, or in the Chancel, where Morning and Evening Prayer are appointed to be said. And the Priest standing at the north side of the Table shall say the Lord's Prayer, with the Collect following, the people kneeling.[22]

And, as Bosher says, while some Bishops wanted the Durham Book used as a model for a revised Prayer Book, this did not happen.[23] So the *Book of Common Prayer* of 1662 was largely the Book of 1552, a conservative, Protestant, and Reformed choice. The 1552 Book had been in use since that year in its original form or 1559 version except during the reign of Mary. That revised book formed the basis for the 1662 Book. That is scarcely a sign of even a mild Counter-Reformation!

And as Bosher informs us, even Bishops like Sheldon and Cosin held ordinations just before August 25th to include those who wanted to be ordained,[24] and 'the bishops exerted themselves by individual persuasion to keep a conforming Puritan party in the

---

[21] C. Neill and J.M. Willoughby, *The Tutorial Prayer Book,* (London: Church Book Room Press, 1959), pp. 291-297.
[22] This is one of the introductory rubrics in the Holy Communion service in the 1662 *Book of Common Prayer.*
[23] Bosher, *Restoration Settlement,* pp. 246-248.
[24] Bosher, *Restoration Settlement,* p. 272.

Church'.[25] Even though he uses 'Laudian' in the title of the book, he admits that it is an unsatisfactory description of the style of the 1662 Restoration.[26]

The re-introduction of the *Thirty-Nine Articles* as part of the Restoration settlement was another sign of its Reformed theology and conservative attitude.[27] These Articles were based on Cranmer's Articles of 1553, which were revised to form the *Thirty-Nine Articles* of 1571. The 1662 Settlement included as its primary documents the Prayer Book of 1552, with some amendments, and the Articles of 1571. It was a conservative and Reformed Settlement.

It is significant that Martyn Lloyd-Jones used Bosher to support his view that the Church of England after 1662 was not in any respect a Puritan church.[28] He argued that the mistakes of the Puritans were those of mixing religion and politics, endless internal divisions, and attempting to be a state church.[29] Bosher wrote his book to demonstrate that the 1662 Settlement

---

[25] Bosher, *Restoration Settlement*, p. 282.

[26] Bosher, *Restoration Settlement* , p. xv. 'Laudian' refers to the High-Church and Arminian William Laud, Archbishop of Canterbury from 1633-1645. See also Julian Davies, *The Caroline captivity of the church: Charles I and the Remoulding of Anglicanism 1625-1641*, (Oxford: Clarendon Press, 1992), pp. 46-86.

[27] See on the *Thirty-Nine Articles*: Gerald Bray, *The Faith We Confess*, (London: The Latimer Trust, 2009); D.B. Knox, *The Thirty-Nine Articles: The historic basis of Anglican Faith*, (London: Hodder and Stoughton, 1967); Oliver O'Donovan, *On the Thirty-Nine Articles: A Conversation with Tudor Christianity*, (Exeter: Paternoster Press, 1993); Ashley Null, *The Thirty-Nine Articles and Reformation Anglicanism*, (Mukono: Uganda Christian University, 2005); James I. Packer, *The Thirty-Nine Articles: their Place and Use Today*, (Vancouver: Regent College Publishing, 2007); J.C. Ryle, 'The Church's distinctive principles', in *Principles for Churchmen*, (London: C.J. Thynne, 1900) pp. 1-30; W.H. Griffith Thomas, *The Principles of Theology: An Introduction to the Thirty-Nine Articles*, (Oregon: Wipf and Stock Publishers, 2005).

[28] D. Martyn Lloyd-Jones [ed.], *The Puritans: Their Origins and Successors, Addresses Delivered at the Puritan and Westminster Conferences, 1959-1978*, (Edinburgh: Banner of Truth, 1987), pp. 57,58.

[29] Lloyd-Jones, *Puritans*, pp. 61-63.

represented a Laudian Church of England. Lloyd-Jones used Bosher because he wants to claim that Puritans do not belong in the Church of England.

The identity of Anglicans in 1662 is important, because many take this to be the defining moment of Anglicanism. In the words of Diarmaid MacCulloch, 'Now there was a Church of England which could be described as 'Anglican'.[30] If he is right, it was Reformed Anglicanism.

Furthermore that Act and that *Book of Common Prayer* defined the Church of England for three hundred years, and formed many parts of global Anglicanism, even reaching the Antipodes. The liturgical style of taking the North End of the Table for the Holy Communion continued for two hundred years, until the Oxford movement of the Nineteenth Century began its liturgical revisions. The long shadow of the 1552 Prayer Book, reinforced by the 1662 Prayer Book is seen in that John Henry Newman, when Vicar of St Mary Magdalene Oxford, celebrated Holy Communion at the North End of the Holy Table, dressed in surplice, scarf, and academic hood.[31]

And the 1662 *Book of Common Prayer, Ordinal* and *Thirty-Nine Articles* still form the doctrinal centre of the Church of England. Canon A5 of the Church of England reads:

> The doctrine of the Church of England is grounded in the Holy Scriptures, and in such teachings of the Ancient Fathers and Councils of the Church as are agreeable to the said Scriptures.

---

[30] MacCulloch, *Reformation,* p. 530. However, against Bosher, he states that 'it could never be the Church that Laud wanted...' p. 530.
[31] Withey, Donald A., *John Henry Newman: The Liturgy and the Breviary,* (London: Sheed and Ward, 1992), p. 12.

In particular such Doctrine is found in the Thirty-Nine Articles of Religion, The Book of Common Prayer, and the Ordinal.[32]

The same doctrinal identity is expressed in Canon C15, 'Of the Declaration of Assent':

> The Church of England is part of the One, Holy, Catholic and Apostolic Church worshipping the one true God, Father, Son and Holy Spirit. It professes the faith uniquely revealed in the Holy Scriptures and set forth in the catholic creeds, which faith the Church is called upon to proclaim afresh in each generation. Led by the Holy Spirit, it has borne witness to Christian truth in its historic formularies, the Thirty-Nine Articles of Religion, The Book of Common Prayer and the Ordering of Bishops, Priests and Deacons. In the declaration you are about to make will you affirm your loyalty to this inheritance of faith as your inspiration and guidance under God in bringing the grace and truth of Christ to this generation and making him known to those in your care?[33]

Stephen Sykes has noted that this is not just important for members of the Church of England, but also significant for all who claim to be Anglicans:

> The Book of Common Prayer, the Thirty-Nine Articles, and the Ordering of Bishops, Priests and Deacons....constitute what in the Church of England is spoken of as its "inheritance of faith" [see Canon C15]...insofar as they define the faith inheritance of the See of Canterbury, and insofar as communion with that See defines what it means to be to belong to the Anglican Communion, these documents have significant authority among Anglicans

---

[32]   The Canons of the Church of England. http://www.churchofengland.org/about-us/structure/churchlawlegis/canons/canons-7th-edition.aspx

[33]   The Canons.

throughout the world.[34]

So 1662 is a key to Anglican identity. In my booklet, *The 'Very pure Word of God': the Book of Common Prayer as a model of Biblical Liturgy*,[35] I have tried to show that the 1662 Prayer Book is a good example of Biblical and Reformed Liturgy, as befits a constitutionally Biblical and Reformed Church.

Some Anglicans and some Nonconformists may want to deny the Reformed identity of Anglicanism, but both are mistaken. As it was defined by 1662, it remained an English Reformed church, and it continued to include Reformed ministers and ministry. From another perspective, Paul Zahl points out that the English Reformation lasted 170 years, from 1520 to 1690, and resulted in 'a Protestant Reformed Church and a Protestant Reformed nation'.[36]

However despite its Reformed identity expressed in the *Book of Common Prayer,* the *Ordinal,* and the *Thirty-Nine Articles,* it was often less than Reformed in fact. By the time the boundaries of the Church had been stretched and extended by the Arminians and Latitudinarians in the 17th Century, the Evangelical Revival and the Oxford Movement in the 18th and 19th Centuries, and by Liberal Theology, and by Quaker spirituality in the 20th Century, it had become a far more comprehensive church than Oliver Cromwell could have imagined.

Nevertheless, Reformed and Evangelical Anglicans continued to belong to it, and valued its good heritage. Frank Lambert shows how George Whitefield, Reformed Anglican leader of the Evangelical Revival in England and North America, was

---

[34] Stephen Sykes, 'The Anglican Character', in Ian Bunting, [ed.], *Celebrating the Anglican Way,* (London: Hodder and Stoughton, 1996), p. 23.
[35] Peter Adam, *The 'Very Pure Word of God': the Book of Common Prayer as a Model of Biblical Liturgy,* (London: The Latimer Trust, 2012).
[36] Paul F.M. Zahl, *The Protestant Face of Anglicanism,* (Grand Rapids/Cambridge: Eerdmans, 1998), p. 27.

influenced by Episcopal and nonconformist Puritans, such as William Perkins, Henry Scougal, William Burkitt, Richard Baxter, and John Bunyan.[37] Augustus Toplady was an active defended of the Reformed identity of the Church of England.[38] Most of the Anglican clergy of the Evangelical Revival felt that they belonged in the Church of England, and were happy to use its Prayer Book. So John Wesley wrote,

> I believe there is no Liturgy in the world, either in ancient or modern language, which breathes more of a solid, scriptural, rational piety than the Common Prayer of the Church of England.[39]

The nineteenth Century Evangelical leader Charles Simeon preached 'On the Excellence of the Liturgy' (that is, the *Book of Common Prayer)*, and had a high estimation of the value that Book. He claimed: 'The finest sight short of heaven would be a whole congregation using the prayers of the Liturgy in the true spirit of them'.[40] He recognized the practical superiority of 'precomposed' prayers:

> If all men could pray at all times as some men can sometimes, then indeed we might prefer extempore to precomposed prayers.[41]

After a visit to Scotland, and the experience of much extempore

---

[37] Frank Lambert, *'Pedlar in Divinity': George Whitefield and the Transatlantic Revivals,* (Princeton: Princeton University Press, 1994), pp. 17-21.

[38] See Toplady, 'Historical Proof', and Gatiss, *True Profession.*

[39] From 'The Preface to John Wesley's Prayer Book', in *The Sunday Service of the Methodists in North America,* James F. White, [ed.], (Cleveland: OSL Publications, 1991).

[40] Hugh Evan Hopkins, *Charles Simeon of Cambridge,* (London: Hodder and Stoughton, 1977), pp. 42,43. And see also Andrew Atherstone, *Charles Simeon on "The Excellency of the Liturgy",* (Norwich: Canterbury Press, 2012).

[41] Hopkins, *Simeon,* p. 213.

prayer, he commented: 'Thank God we have a Liturgy'.[42]

4.1.2   A conservative and repressive church

Though the Restoration looked like triumph for the King, the Bishops, and the traditional Anglicans, it was a pyrrhic victory. The real power was in the Parliament, not the King or the Bishops. The new King, King James II, who succeeded Charles II was defeated in the Glorious Revolution of 1689, and replaced by William and Mary. Whereas Charles I had been tried and executed by the Commonwealth,[43] James was replaced by members of an Anglican Parliament. Bishops were reinstated, but with limited power, as the terms of the Settlement were decided by Parliament, and there was no particular theology of the Episcopate included in the Settlement.[44] The King and the Bishops appeared to have power, but did not. Furthermore the conservatism of the Anglican reaction expressed in 1662 led to a fossilized Church of England, where change became difficult.[45] This conservatism was increased by the suspension and then eclipse of Convocation from 1664, which meant that only the Parliament could change the Church of England.[46]

As we have seen, more ministers of Reformed convictions remained in the Church than left it. Yet the Church of England suffered from the conservatism of the 1662 Settlement, which was an attempt to reinstate and recover the pre-Commonwealth past, not an attempt to find appropriate renewal and life for the future. The restrictions of 1662 cast a long shadow. The Church was

---

[42]   Hopkins, *Simeon*, p. 190.
[43]   See Geoffrey Robinson, *The Tyrannicide Brief: The Story of the Man who sent Charles I to the Scaffold*, (London: Vintage, 2006).
[44]   Paul Avis, *Anglicanism and the Christian Church*, (Edinburgh: T&T Clark, 1989), pp. 306-311.
[45]   Hutton, *Restoration*, pp. 181-193; Chadwick, *Reformation*, p. 247; and Green, *Religion*, p. 153-175.
[46]   Sykes, *Sheldon*, pp. 36-67. Convocation was a meeting of representative clergy of the Church of England.

subject to Parliament for its constitution, and dependent on the monarch for the appointment of bishops and deans. It was a strongly conformist church. So the Evangelical Charles Simeon was wary of praying at meetings of undergraduates whom he prepared for ordination in his rooms in King's College Cambridge in the 19th Century, lest he fall foul of the Conventicle Act, which prohibited religious meetings: 'I would not do anything which might subject me to the Conventicle Act.'[47] And services at the Anglican Church I attended in Melbourne in the 1950s included only set prayers from the *Book of Common Prayer*. As we have seen, the primary documents of 1662 were based on Cranmer's 1552 Prayer Book and 1553 Articles, as revised in 1571. The 1662 settlement was based on Reformed Anglicanism of the 1550s, and lasted without change until the liturgical revisions of the late 20th Century.

Nonconformists were further repressed during the reign of Queen Anne. And the restrictions placed on nonconformists and Roman Catholics remained in place until the Nineteenth Century, not least in that they were not allowed to graduate from universities.

And 1662 produced Nonconformist churches, comprising those ministers and people who had refused to submit to Anglican regulations. In the words of Diarmaid MacCulloch, 'By their hard-line stance, the Anglicans created 'Dissent' out of those who had been part of the united pre-war Church of England.'[48] In a sense, the Civil War continued. The Puritans had been successful until 1660, and now the Anglicans were winning. But the Civil War only ended with the toleration of dissent in 1689: this was 'the real end of the civil war'.[49] This now meant that nation and church were not co-extensive, and that the Church of England no longer represented the nation.

---

[47] H.C.G. Moule, *Charles Simeon*, (London: Inter-Varsity Fellowship, 1956), p. 145.
[48] MacCulloch, *Reformation*, p. 531.
[49] Hutton, *Restoration*, p. 290.

4.1.3   A weak church

What of the conversion of England? Keith Thomas has argued that even in the Medieval church,

> the hold of organized religion upon the people was never so complete as to leave no room for rival systems of belief.[50]

Lack of belief in Christianity continued through the 16th and 17th Centuries,[51] and accounts of the Evangelical Revival that began in the 1730s indicate that neither Anglicans nor Nonconformists had been vastly effective in preaching the gospel in England after 1662.

Some might have expected that a restored Church of England, now purified by the dismissal of inferior ministers would flourish. That did not happen. Though it continued constitutionally as an orthodox and Reformed church, it was weakened by Arminian anti-Reformed ideas and practices by theologically indifferent Latitudinarianism, by Deism, by Arianism, and by Unitarianism. Though there was an effective defence of Trinitarian orthodoxy within the Church, it did not find expression in effective gospel ministry.

While Reformed Anglicanism continued after the Restoration, as Stephen Hampton has shown, it was so conformist that it lost its cutting edge. So Hampton cites Seth Ward, Bishop of Exeter and then Salisbury as a Reformed Anglican.[52] Yet in 1662 Ward wrote of the 'clergy-presbyters' of his diocese as: 'enemies of the Church', of whom he desired 'an universal riddance at once'.[53] Those whom he should have loved as brothers in the gospel he dismissed because of their lack of Anglican order. Valuing conformity to church practice over gospel partnership is a great sin.

---

[50]   Keith Thomas, *Religion and the Decline of Magic,* (London: Penguin, 1991), p. 206.
[51]   Thomas, *Religion*, pp. 179-206.
[52]   Hampton, *Anti-Arminians*, p. 17.
[53]   Quoted in Sykes, *Sheldon*, p. 69.

It is possible to be orthodox but ineffective in ministry and evangelism. As the Lutheran Church needed the Pietists, including the Moravians, and as the Reformed Church needed the 'second reformation',[54] so the Church of England needed the Evangelical Revival. The interview between Bishop Butler and John Wesley is instructive, as it demonstrates how far the Bishop had fallen from understanding the nature of saving faith in Christ. In the words of the Bishop, 'Why, Sir, our faith itself is a good work; it is a virtuous temper of mind.'[55]

It is also instructive to see why the Anglican clergy of the Evangelical Revival were often rejected and persecuted by the Church of England.

Firstly there was a fear of 'enthusiasm'. In Bishop Butler's words to John Wesley: 'Sir, the pretending to extraordinary revelations and gifts of the Holy Ghost is a horrid thing, a very horrid thing'.[56]

Claims to be directed by God, and the presence of physical signs of distress and joy by those who heard sermons were reminiscent of the behaviour of the Quakers, and an offense to rational and reasonable religion. In Bishop Butler's words: 'I hear, too, that many people fall into fits in your societies, and that you pray over them'.[57]

Secondly there was a theological objection to the gospel of grace. It was feared that grace would lead to antinomianism, to sin. Even the theological explanation of grace found in the *Thirty-Nine Articles,* and expressed in the *Book of Common Prayer* and the

---

[54] See Joel R. Beeke, 'Evangelicalism and the Dutch Further Reformation', in Michael A.G. Haykin and Kenneth J. Stewart, [eds.], *The Emergence of Evangelicalism: Exploring Historical Continuities,* (Nottingham: Apollos, 2008), pp. 146-168.

[55] John Wesley, *The Journal of John Wesley,* Volume Two, Nehemiah Curnock [ed.], (London: Epworth Press, 1938), p. 256.

[56] Wesley, *Journal,* p. 257.

[57] Wesley, *Journal,* p. 257.

book of Homilies was no defence.[58]

Thirdly, preaching outside Church buildings and breaking parish boundaries was also condemned. Here is Bishop Butler again addressing Wesley:

> You have not business here. You are not commissioned to preach in this diocese. Therefore I advise you to go hence.[59]

The Anglican clergy who did not respect parish boundaries were operating as nonconformists. From another perspective, they were reviving the ministry of the Medieval preaching orders, who had been founded to bring the gospel, but who had not been constrained by parish boundaries. The loss of the preaching orders and monasteries had left the parishes and dioceses as the only structure of Anglican ministry except for cathedrals and university chapels, and this made rectors and vicars of parishes keen to maintain their boundaries.

In terms of evangelising England, the closure of the monasteries and the closure of the preaching orders at the time of the Reformation meant that the parish system was left to carry the burden of evangelisation. However the parish system had already beginning to fail by the 13th Century. That was why two complementary missional models flourished in order to fill the gaps, namely the convent or monastery as a base of local mission and ministry (as had been the practice in the native Celtic Church), and the peripatetic preaching orders, such as the Franciscans and Dominicans. The Methodists were the new preaching orders.

Some Evangelical clergy, such as Charles Simeon, were careful to minister within Anglican rules, as we have seen, while others, like William Grimshaw of Haworth combined very effective

---

[58] Wesley, *Journal*, p. 257.
[59] Wesley, *Journal*, p. 257.

ministry in their own parishes with wider ministries beyond.[60]

Many gospel ministers of the Evangelical Revival did value the Reformed theological identity of Anglicanism expressed in the 1662 *Book of Common Prayer* and the *Thirty-Nine Articles*, and felt that this was their ecclesiastical home. This has continued until the present, and also continues today in global Anglicanism.

4.2 For the nonconformists

4.2.1 Persecution and suffering

Great suffering was the result.[61] Ministers lost their ministries, in some cases lost their congregations, and lost their incomes. Members of churches lost beloved ministers. Then ministers and their people were persecuted, fined, and imprisoned under increasingly oppressive Acts of Parliament, and often under oppressive judges and magistrates. The 1662 Act of Uniformity and the 1665 File Mile Act related to ministers: the Conventicle Acts of 1664 and 1670 were directed at congregations.

Meeting houses were torn down, congregations dispersed, funerals attacked, and legal trials perverted. At one of Richard Baxter's trials, Judge Jefferys forbad Baxter and his lawyer to present their defence, and anticipated the verdict of the jury. At the trial of two Quakers, William Penn and Matthew Mead, the Magistrate told the jurors that 'you will not be dismissed till we have a verdict that the court will accept; and you shall be locked up, without meat, drink, fire, and tobacco...we will have a verdict by the help of God or you shall starve for it'.[62] There was some relief from the harsher penalties in 1672, and more with the Toleration Act of

---

[60] Frank Baker, *William Grimshaw 1708-1763*, (London: Epworth Press, 1963), pp. 90-114, 144-161, 175-188.

[61] Cragg, *Puritanism, Persecution*, chapters II-IV, and Spurr, 'Puritanism to Dissent', pp. 247-257.

[62] As quoted in Cragg, *Puritanism, Persecution*, pp. 49.

1689. But it had still been a time of 'Great Persecution'.

One might have thought that such refining suffering and persecution would result in great gospel growth and blessing among nonconformists, but that was not the case. As John Spurr wrote, 'Life "under the cross" brought the usual problems attendant on persecution – suffering, evasion, compromise...'.[63]

4.2.2 Divisions and weakness

Nonconformists were about 2% of the population in 1670.[64] Unfortunately they continued to suffer from divisions. Not only were they divided between Presbyterians, Independents, Baptists and others, but these groups were themselves divided. So the Baptists in 1660 were divided between 110 Calvinist or 'Particular' congregations, and 130 Arminian or 'General' congregations. Some 'Strict' Baptist congregations restricted participation in the Lord's Supper to members of the congregation, while others allowed members of other congregations to participate. Some Calvinist Baptists became Hyper-Calvinist. Some were 'Seventh-Day' Baptists, and met on Saturdays, while others met on Sundays.[65] And while many Baptists were strict on the matter of baptism, the notable John Bunyan placed less emphasis on its necessity.[66]

The Presbyterians were also divided: some had conformed, while others had not. Those who did not conform were divided between those who hankered after participation in the national church and so were reluctant to start new congregations, and those who had given up hope of a comprehensive national church, and so were ready to start new churches.[67] Nonconforming

[63] Spurr, 'Puritanism to Dissent', p. 234.
[64] Spurr, *Post-Reformation*, p. 132.
[65] Spurr, 'Puritanism to Dissent', p. 240.
[66] Hill, *Turbulent*, 292-295.
[67] Spurr, 'Puritanism to Dissent', p. 246.

Presbyterians were divided between Calvinism and Arminianism,[68] and there was also a significant group of 'Moderates', including Philip Doddridge and Isaac Watts.[69] Some nonconformists were deeply distressed at being accused of schism, including Richard Baxter and John Owen. Baxter continued his attempts to bring about a more comprehensive Church of England, and Owen wrote a theological defence of the nonconformists' actions, pointing to the sin of causing schism by placing unnecessary restrictions on others, or by changing the faith.[70] At one stage Richard Baxter argued for a comprehensive church with only the Apostles' Creed, the Lord's Prayer, and the Ten Commandments as 'our Essentials or Fundamentals'.[71] This would have been a remarkably broad church.

While in due course the Evangelical Revival which began in the 1730s brought new life to nonconformist churches, their first reaction was negative. George Whitefield was as critical of nonconformists as he was of the Church of England.[72]

For the nonconformists there was no immediate revival after 1662. It was a time of decline and decay, though also a time of faithful gospel ministry under great trial.[73]

4.3 For Anglicans and nonconformists

The departure of 1760 ministers in 1662 meant of course the parting of friends, as some conformed, and some did not.

---

[68] Spurr, 'Puritanism to Dissent', p. 256, and for a later similar division, Field, *Howe*, p. 179.

[69] Field, *Howe*, pp. 18-29, 179.

[70] On Baxter, see Wood, *Church unity*, pp. 241-262, and on John Owen, *The Works of John Owen, Volumes 13-15*, (London: Banner of Truth, 1966 {1850-53}).

[71] Geoffrey F. Nuttall, *Richard Baxter*, (London: Nelson, 1965), p. 122.

[72] D.W. Bebbington, *Evangelicalism in Modern Britain: A History from the 1730s to the 1980s*, (London: Unwin Hyman, 1989), pp. 21-23.

[73] Bebbington, *Evangelicalism* p. 21, and Poole-Connor, *Evangelicalism*, pp. 139-148.

Ministers who stayed and ministers who left would both have felt this to be a gospel trial. This was a particular issue for Presbyterians, who were the group closest to Anglicanism in their theology of the church and ministry. It was painful to see gospel ministry divided, and to lose the possibility of close association in ministry. And congregations suffered, as some lost beloved ministers, and some congregations were divided as some members stayed and others left.

However sometimes ministers with compatible ideas did support each other across the new divide. We have already seen the benefits of a shared commitment to Biblical exposition. We also find a common use of the *Book of Common Prayer*. Henry Havers, Rector of Stambourne, in Essex resigned in 1662, continued his ministry, and built a meeting house, which he licensed as a Presbyterian Meeting House in 1672. After theological confusion affected the Presbyterians, it became Independent. And this church used parts of the 1662 *Book of Common Prayer* at least until 1735,

> Up to this time [1735] – and how long after is now known – The Book of Common Prayer was used in the worship, showing that although the founders could not subscribe their assent and consent to everything contained therein, they did not discard the whole book on that account, but continued to use those portions of it which they found to be helpful and edifying.[74]

There were close connections between Anglicans and nonconformists in some places.

However for both Anglicans and nonconformists the period after 1662 was not a time of very effective ministry, for a number of reasons, as we have seen. The Evangelical Revival which

---

[74] Charles Haddon Spurgeon, *Memories of Stambourne*, (Pasadena: Pilgrim, 1975), p. 44. One of its later ministers was James Spurgeon, grandfather of Charles Spurgeon.

began in the 1730s demonstrated large-scale ignorance of the gospel both within the churches and throughout the nation. It also revived and renewed both the Church of England and nonconformist ministry, and of course added the Methodists as a new nonconformist church.

It is difficult to think of a Biblical instruction to leave a church or to leave ministry in a church because it has fallen away from the gospel. Jeremiah had to continue his ministry, and face the consequent persecution. Timothy seems to be the only minister in Ephesus, or indeed in Asia (presumably the Roman Province of Asia) who was still faithful to Paul's gospel, but he was instructed to stay, teach, and reform.

However it is not possible for us to decide whether it was right to stay in 1662 or to go. It is not for us to judge, for each person is accountable to God for their own actions. There were no doubt many different reasons for staying, and many different motivations for leaving.

Thomas Lye, in his final sermon, included these revealing and wise words:

> [i]n these present days, we will often hear it said, so-and-so cannot be an honest man for he does not conform: or, on the other hand, he cannot be an honest man, because he does conform...I cannot in conscience conform...could I conform without sin to my conscience, I would...Do not then spend the strength of your zeal for your religion in censuring others.[75]

John Whitlock gave his congregation this advice: 'If sound truth be powerfully preached, make use of, and improve that, though you cannot approve of everything the minister does.'[76] And he wisely warned his people not to be too quick to judge ministers:

---

[75]   As quoted in Murray, *Sermons*, p. 102.
[76]   As quoted in Murray, *Sermons*, p. 193.

I know while the best of men are on earth, there is likely to be a variety of apprehensions; and some men of sound judgment in the main, may satisfy themselves in the lawfulness of some things that others find sinful...[77]

Matthew Newcomen, Vicar of Dedham, was one who resigned in 1662. In his final sermon, he preached these words:

It hath been all along, a Merciful Providence of God, that when some of his servants could not satisfy their consciences, and come up to the things that have been imposed upon them, without injuring their Consciences; yet others have had a greater freedom given them, that they could yield: and if not so, what would have become of the people of God? Therefore, in those things, achieved there may be some providence of God, for good to you be in it.[78]

So in trusting God's providential care, he recognized that it was the good plan of God for some ministers to stay and for some to leave.

This booklet is dedicated to those who stayed for the sake of Christ and the gospel, and to those who left, for the sake of Christ and the gospel. They honoured God by patiently enduring gospel trials, and by their lives and ministries. May their examples encourage us to fight the good fight, keep the faith, and run and race, so that we, with them, may receive the crown.

And Thomas Brooks, in his farewell sermon, expressed a hope for the future blessings of God:

There may be an hour of darkness that may be upon the gospel, as to its liberty, purity and glory; and yet there may be a sunshining day ready to tread on the heels of it.[79]

---

[77] As quoted in Murray, *Sermons*, p. 194.
[78] As quoted in Anne Whiteman, 'The Restoration of the Church of England', pp. 21-88, in Geoffrey F. Nuttall and Owen Chadwick, *From Uniformity to Unity, 1662-1962*, (London: SPCK, 1962), p.21.
[79] As quoted in Murray, *Sermons*, p. 43.

5. What wisdom can we find for this kind of situation?

We will not find ourselves in exactly the same situation as that faced in 1662. History does not repeat itself exactly. However reflecting on what happened may prompt us to ask if, in a similar situation, we would stay or go. As we think on these things, here are some Biblical and theological issues, and then some practical advice.

5.1 Biblical and theological issues

5.1.1 A holy church?

> To the church of God in Corinth, to those sanctified in Christ Jesus and called to be his holy people.[1]

Paul, the great missionary to the nations, spent a lot of energy caring for, reforming and renewing the churches. Though the church at Corinth was deep in sin, he did not write to it as if it was no longer a church. It is 'the church of God in Corinth' and it is made up of those who are 'sanctified in Christ Jesus,' even if some if not the majority are sinful. The church is justified and sanctified by grace, just as individuals are justified and sanctified by grace. We must not fall into the trap of rejoicing in God's grace for ourselves, but denying it to others or to the church. And Paul did not instruct Timothy, an elder at the corrupt church at Ephesus to leave it and start again, but to stay and reform. Richard Baxter's words are important:

> ...know that all men are imperfect and faulty, and so is all Men's Worship of God; and he that will not communicate with faulty worship must renounce communion with all

---

[1] 1 Corinthians 1:2.

the World.[2]

As John Flavel wrote: 'O be not too quick to bury the Church before she is dead.'[3]

5.1.2   Strengths and weaknesses

> So, if you think you are standing firm, be careful that you don't fall![4]

One painful feature of humanity is that every strength has a weakness attached to it, and every good gift may be misused. Theological clarity can lead to intolerance, theological generosity can lead to indifference, individual responsibility can lead to pride, and conformity can lead to compromise. What were the strengths of the Puritans, of enthusiastically Reformed Christians? They were Biblical, focused on individual responsibility, they were committed to congregations, they were urgent for the reform of the church and the reform of the nation. But all these strengths made them divisive in character, which weakened them internally, and diminished their effect on others. Their demise in England in the 17th Century was perhaps an inevitable result of precisianism, individualism, congregationalism, and the refusal to allow any action or belief to be of secondary importance, in which a variety of opinions could be allowed.

5.1.3   The role of the Bible

> Sanctify them by the truth; your word is truth.[5]

There was a significant distinction between other Puritans and Reformed Anglicans. Other Puritans required that churches only

---

[2]   Quoted in the introduction to Baxter, *Autobiography*, p. xxii, (from Baxter's *'Sacrilegious Desertion...Rebuked'* of 1672).
[3]   John Flavel, as quoted in I.D.E. Thomas, *A Puritan Golden Treasury*, (Edinburgh: Banner of Truth, 1977), p. 58.
[4]   1 Corinthians 10:12.
[5]   John 17:17.

engage in practices commanded in the Bible, and objected to non-Biblical practices within the Church of England. The Anglican Reformed use of the Bible was significantly different. It held that to be Biblical meant to conform to Biblical doctrine, and included in that category consequences and expressions of Biblical truth. It opposed and precluded un-Biblical and anti-Biblical ideas and practices. It was not restricted to only obeying express instructions of Scripture, but could do and say things not prescribed in Scripture, as long as they expressed Bible truth, and did not contradict it, and as long as everything was done for edification.[6]

This view reflects ordinary life, in which we do not limit ourselves to only doing what the Bible tells us to do. If we followed this exactly, we would not send our children to school, get interest on the money in our bank accounts, or consider adopting children. Furthermore in our services we would not give notices or take up a collection for the work of the church: and we would enrol all widows! Furthermore, all churches have to develop disciplines and patterns in order to function, and not all of these come directly from the Bible. And even those Puritans who agreed that the polity and practice of the church should come directly from the Bible could not agree on what the Bible commanded. Presbyterians, Independents and Baptists all made the same claim but did not agree on polity or practice. As a matter of fact, there is little instruction about the expected polity or practice of the church after the age of the apostles in the New Testament. And, as we have seen, there is no command to leave a church or denomination. And how could one justify a series of sermons on the Westminster Catechism, such as those preached by Thomas Watson? While

---

[6] For more on this see my *Very pure Word*, pp. 32 and 61, and see also Trevor Lloyd, 'Worship and the Bible', in Colin Buchanan, Trevor Lloyd and Harold Miller, [eds.], *Anglican Worship Today*, (London: Collins, 1980), pp. 14-19. From a different perspective, see D.A. Carson, [ed.], *Worship by the Book*, (Grand Rapids: Zondervan, 2002), pp. 11-63; and D.G. Hart and John R. Mueller, *With Reverence and Awe: Returning to the Basics of Reformed Worship*, (Philippsburg: P&R, 2002), pp. 89-102, 145-158.

each sermon begins with a Bible text, the words of the Catechism were the real text that was expounded.[7]

However, the Bible is central to the 1662 *Book of Common Prayer*, the *Ordinal*, and the *Thirty-Nine Articles*, and Anglicans are called to be thoroughly Biblical, without needing to find specific Biblical justification for all their actions.

5.1.4 Patience in ministry

Love is patient...the fruit of the Spirit is love, joy, peace, patience.[8]

How difficult it is for ministers who are urgent for change, urgent for the holiness of God's people, urgent for God's glory, not to provoke people in their care. We want them to change, and see such little progress, such slow transformation. We need patience with individuals, much more patience with a congregation, and even more patience with a denomination or nation. When we have high standards for ourselves, it is difficult not to set high standards for others. Yet as conscientious parents are in danger of provoking their children, and driving them to discouragement or rebellion, we need to learn love, patience, sympathy and hope in our ministry! The Puritans had high standards for themselves, their ministries, their families, their churches, their communities, and their nation. Perhaps they needed wisdom in not provoking people by demanding of them more gospel growth than they were able to deliver.

5.1.5 Welcome one another

One person considers one day more sacred than another; another considers every day alike. Each of them should be fully convinced in their own mind. So whatever you believe

---

[7] Watson, *Divinity.*
[8] 1 Corinthians 13: 4, Galatians 5:22.

about these things keep between yourself and God...Accept one another, then, just as Christ accepted you, in order to bring praise to God.[9]

If I had been writing Romans, I would have told those who were weak in faith, and still kept special days, to sort themselves out, and to know that they are justified by grace through faith, not by keeping special days of Jewish practice. Paul, on the other hand, told the strong in faith to accept the weak in faith, and the weak in faith to accept the strong in faith. Both the strong and the weak are answerable to God, not to each other. So we must allow people to act differently in matters that don't contradict the gospel.

The Church of England was certainly too tough in the regulations they imposed in 1662 and the ways they imposed them. It was right to complain that the Church was being unduly particular on secondary matters. But then those who did not conform were also being particular about secondary matters. And some more precise Puritans believed that there were no matters of secondary importance. This is unrealistic as every congregation needs rules to govern its behaviour, and members need love and forbearance in many matters. If we want to find total agreement in everything, we will have very small churches! And Paul does allow for mutually accepting differences in practice in Romans 14 and 15, as we have seen.

The Puritans were known as 'Precisianists', because, as we have seen, they served a precise God. What happened in 1662 was that some Puritan 'precisianists' came into conflict with Anglican 'precisianism'. One of my daily prayers includes two requests: that God would stop me confusing gospel progress with a desire to get my own way, and that God would stop me from turning personal preferences into rigorous principles! Divisiveness is a sin,[10] and it is a sin which we are liable to commit because of our instinctive

---

[9] Romans 14:5,22 and 15:7.
[10] 1 Corinthians 1, Galatians 5:20.

individualism and commitment to our rights. Necessary division should be a matter of deep grief, not of the enjoyment of power.

Please remember that leaving need not imply that the church you are leaving is no longer a church of Jesus Christ, or that it is a lost cause. We should resist the temptation to inflate the theology in order to justify the actions.

5.2 Practical advice

History does not repeat itself, so we could not be the same situation as people faced in 1662. However reflecting on what happened may prompt us to ask if, in a similar situation, we would stay or go. Here is some further wisdom, as we reflect on what happened then.

5.2.1 Don't have unrealistic expectations

One might have expected that great gospel growth and revival would be the result of the costly decision of so many gospel ministers to leave the Church of England. It did not. They eventually gained their freedom to do their own ministries in their own ways, but did not meet great success. I say this not to diminish the way they honoured God under trial and persecution, but as a warning that leaving does not always result in growth and revival.

Similarly in the next Century, during the Evangelical revival, some left the Church of England, and formed new associations of ministry like the Countess of Huntingdon's Connection, and the Methodist Church. This policy enabled growth in the short-term, but ultimately produced its own problems. Both the Countess of Huntingdon's Connection and Whitefield's Calvinistic Methodists eventually collapsed, as we have seen. The Methodists continue, but in the long term faced the same problems as other denominations.

Others remained loyally within the Church of England, and people like Charles Simeon had immense gospel influence despite initial gospel opposition from the people of his church of Holy Trinity Cambridge. However Simeon worked hard to create new models of ministry, to train up future leaders, and to create new structures of ministry within the Church of England and also in cooperation with evangelicals in other churches. If you look from the perspective of the 21st Century, it could be argued that staying within the Church of England had as much gospel impact on the nation as leaving.

5.2.2   Distinguish between church and para-church

It is worth making a distinction between churches and para-church ministries. Churches welcome everyone, and have a wide range of ministries. Para-church organisations have a special target group of people to serve, and a special target ministry to do.

Para-church ministries are often based on the voluntary society principle which has been present in the church from early days. It was found in many 'grass-roots' movements, started by lay people and or clergy with a variety of aims. Some began as holiness movements protecting against the low standards of the churches, and exemplifying a higher standard of Christian discipleship. Some had specialized missional aims or special tasks: the convert the unevangelised, to engage in world mission, to combat heresy, to engage in education, theology, or social care. Many demanded a high level of sacrifice from their members. Some established home communities, hospices, schools and universities, and some were intentionally peripatetic in life-style.

From the early monastic communities through to the Medieval Church, many voluntary societies began, and many continued their lives and ministries. In Roman Catholic theology, these are described as 'sodalities', in contrast to 'modalities'. In Protestant theology, they are known as 'para-church organizations'.

In practice, para-church organizations sometimes become churches or denominations in the longer-term, such as the Methodists and the Salvation Army. And a student or specialist church plant will inevitably develop into a church with a wider ministry over twenty years. However it is worth making the distinction, as it enables clarity of thought and purpose. And the distinction is also useful, because the New Testament requires churches, while para-church organizations are our inventions for particular purposes. We are required by God to belong to a church: para-church organizations are optional. And leaving a church is a more serious matter than leaving a para-church organization.

Our subject in this booklet is churches, rather than para-churches organizations.

5.2.3   Coping with divisions

However, inevitably there will some who stay and some who decide to leave a church in every age. How should we cope with this with Christian maturity?

(a)   For those planning to leave

i.   Do not leave for trivial reasons

Separation is a serious matter, and for leaders to separate is even more serious, because we are judged with greater strictness, and our actions influence others to a greater extent. It would be a great sin to excuse your leaving by claiming that your church or denomination is no longer part of the church of Jesus Christ, when it is. When John Calvin was advising believers in Roman Catholic countries what to do, he reminded them that, 'the catholic church is spread throughout the countries where the pope's tyranny rules.'[11] And he added,

> ...we have here the sort of church that existed anciently among the Israelites after they became corrupted. So, I would not approve of someone who utterly rejected such a

---

[11]   John Calvin, *Come Out From Among Them: 'Anti-Nicodemite' Writings of John Calvin,* tr. Seth Skolnitsky, (Dallas: Protestant Heritage Press, 2001), p. 39.

people, or excommunicated it by withdrawing from its company. Yet I cannot find much to say for communing fully in what is plainly evil...[12]

Calvin's main message was that believers should not compromise with idolatry, but he did not need to claim that the Roman Church was not part of God's church. He pointed out that some practices were not good, but were still not reasons to leave a church. So candles on the Lord's table were a slight error, perhaps of good origin, but later corrupted.[13] And while he encouraged people to leave the Roman Church, he also instructed those who left not to condemn those who did not leave.[14]

It is also worth pointing out that Paul's instruction in 2 Corinthians 6 to 'come out from among them' is not an instruction to leave a corrupt church or denomination, but to avoid being contaminated with idolatry in the world.

Unnecessary schism is a sin. However it is also a sin to cause schism by abandoning the truth, by failing to apply moral or theological discipline, and by placing unnecessary burdens of conformity. This will result in others having to leave, and is the sin of causing schism.

ii. Leave for good reasons

Here are some reasons that could justify separation, though they do not necessarily require it.

- *You are no longer able to endure the sins and weakness of the church or denomination.*

This is different to the previous point. It is possible to believe that a church or denomination is still part of the church of God, but also to that you can no longer bear to live with its sins and weaknesses,

---

[12] Calvin, *Come out,* p. 40.
[13] Calvin, *Come out,* p. 38.
[14] Calvin, *Come out,* p. 44.

either as a member, or else as a minister. Of course all churches, ministries, denominations and associations have their characteristic sins and weaknesses. Shared sins are those which are most invisible to us, because we are not constantly rebuked by the lifestyle of those in our community. On the contrary, they confirm us in our sin by their sin. But, for example, you may find the sins of being too exclusive easier to cope with than the sins of being too inclusive! If you find the sins and weaknesses of your church or ministry highly offensive, then you must either learn to be gracious and patient or you could consider leaving for another context of ministry.

I frequently advise young people considering overseas mission to compare three or four missionary societies, to find out their style, their strengths and weaknesses, and then make a wise choice. And I advise those considering ministry to make a similar comparison between different denominations, if they are undecided. These exercises are partly designed to help people to see the sins of organisations and denominations, and to decide which sort of sins they can live with. We should all make sure that we know the characteristic sins of our church, denomination or organisation, and lament them, work and pray to bring about repentance and change, oppose them and oppose those who perpetrate them, call those who allow them to account, and pray for God's mercy and transforming grace.

- *There is mission and ministry to be done that cannot be done by this church or denomination.*

William Carey was right to challenge Christians in England to work to bring the gospel to people around the world, and he was right to recognise that this could not be done with a 'means', that is, an organisation to achieve that purpose. He wrote his *Enquiry Into the Obligations of Christians to use means for the Conversion of the Heathens,* which led to the founding of the Baptist Missionary

Society in 1792.[15] This was a recognition that local churches could not do world mission by themselves: a 'means' was needed.

The creation of the Baptist Missionary Society was necessary in order to enable global evangelisation. Similar organisations included the Sunday School Movement (Sabbath School) in the 1780s, to provide basic education for poor children; the London Missionary Society, founded in 1795 by Anglicans, Congregationalists, Presbyterians and Wesleyans, with a focus on missionary work in the Pacific; the Church Missionary Society for Anglican global mission in 1799; and The British and Foreign Bible Society in 1804, to circulate Bibles at home and abroad.

iii. To think about before you leave

Do not leave because distant fields look greener! We feel the pressures of our present situation, and cannot yet imagine the pressures we will endure in a different situation. And realise that the parting of friends is always painful, and there are costs for everyone. Present gospel bonds must be weakened if you move to a new context of ministry. And the two great costs of ministry are first of all investing in building relationships, and then extracting yourself from them.

If you are going to leave a church or denomination or association, look for an existing ministry, association, or denomination, rather than creating a new one.

The examples of useful Societies given above remind us that it is worth considering if the same advantages could not be gained by an informal and supportive fellowship, rather than by requiring people to leave their present structures to join a new structure.

Ensure that any new structure will be effective, with gospel priorities, a clear and effective doctrinal statement, a clear focus on

---

[15]   Walker, *Carey*, pp. 78-103.

primary not secondary issues, and with wise governance and legal and financial provisions, and with a national or global vision.

Recognise that if you do create a new church, it will end up as a new denomination or as part of a new denomination. If you do set up a new denomination, then plan it carefully. At the time of the Evangelical Revival, Wesley's Methodists were well set up, with effective standards, structures, organisation, and leadership. By contrast, George Whitefield's Calvinistic Methodists and the similar Countess of Huntingdon's Connection both collapsed in England, though the Calvinistic Methodists continued in Wales.[16]

Reflect on examples from the Bible. What did Jeremiah do? What did Paul ask Timothy to do? What Biblical justification is there for leaving?[17] If you must go, then go in sorrow rather than in pride.

(b)   If you decide to stay

Is it possible to stay in a church or denomination and reform and renew it? Yes, with sufficient resources, patience, flexibility, prayer and dependence on God, and a long-term plan.

The keys to doing this include, making necessary changes, and letting your denomination catch up eventually. Most reforming movements begin 'from below', and the leaders of the denomination and the denomination as a whole catch up eventually.

If you want to see models of effective change, follow the example of the Oxford movement and Anglican liberal theology since the 1850s. The Oxford Movement made changes in liturgy and ministry in parishes, even when opposed by Bishops. Those who made the changes suffered the consequences of breaking

---

[16]   Bebbington, *Evangelicalism*, pp. 29,30.
[17]   See Thomas Oden, 'Do Not Rashly Tear Asunder: Why the Beleaguered Faithful should stay and reform their churches', *First Things*, April 2012, pp. 40-44.

church law, even to going to prison. The changes were eventually accepted, and are now commonly regarded as normal Anglican practice. Anglican liberal theology has made different kinds of changes, in theology and ministry. Its proponents just went ahead with their theological changes, and have successfully changed the church. The lesson is to make changes, and suffer the consequences, and eventually the Church of England will change too.

Make sure that you distinguish between matters of primary importance and matters of secondary importance, and focus your attention on primary matters. Teach and instruct people so that they make the changes and own the changes. Make the useful distinction that Paul makes in 2 Timothy 2 and 3. In 2 Timothy 2:22-26, he encouraged Timothy to work with all who call on the Lord with a pure heart, and to try to win over his opponents, correcting them with gentleness. That is, his aim must be to win people, not arguments. However in 2 Timothy 3:1-9, he warned Timothy to avoid those false teachers who are corrupt and who are corrupting others.

Of course you will be urgent for change. But recognise that God is patient with you and your sins, and show the same patience with others. And of course it takes many years to change a church from its former ways, and decades to change a denomination.

You should also work to raise up the next generation of leaders for your church and for your denomination, and train them well. The training that people receive before they go to theological college is the most influential training they will ever receive. Invest in it with enthusiasm. Build up good support networks for good people in ministry, create new models of ministry, and transform old models to make them more useful.

5.2.4   Reform your church by the Bible

We always need to be reformed by the Word of God, and all our churches, ministries, associations, and denominations always need to reformed by the Word of God. This need will continue until the day of Christ's return. So whether we stay or leave, we will always have this responsibility.

In my St Antholin's Lecture, *A Church "Halfly Reformed": the Puritan Dilemma*, I showed that the Puritan model of reformation expressed the priorities of Paul for his churches, as found in his letters to Timothy and Titus. Let me now rehearse the twelve ingredients of this model.

i. The Puritans printed Bibles and Christian books: Timothy was told that the Scriptures make us wise for salvation through faith in Jesus Christ, and that he is to use these Scriptures in his preaching and teaching (2 Timothy 3:15-4:2, 1 Timothy 4:13).

ii. They recognized the key role of Preachers of the Word: Titus was told to make up what is lacking and appoint elders for the churches who are of sound moral character, and who are able to teach the truth and correct error (Titus 1:5-9).

iii. They provided Biblical Training of Ministers: Timothy was urged to pass on apostolic words in which the Gospel is preserved by training faithful people who will be able to teach others, and Paul trains by example as well as by instruction (2 Timothy 1:13,14 and 2:2).

iv. They created a new style of Preaching, and worked hard at finding an effective method of communication: Paul urged Timothy to teach with great patience and careful instruction, and to pay attention to his teaching (1 Timothy 4:13, and 2 Timothy 4:2).

v. They provided support and in-service training for Ministers: Paul provided this in 1 and 2 Timothy and Titus, and also appealed for support in his own ministry (2 Timothy 4:9-22).

vi. They created new models and opportunities for ministry: Paul encouraged Timothy to look for new opportunities and to fulfil his ministry (2 Timothy 4:5,9).

vii. They had committed and trained lay people: Titus was told to encourage members of the church to teach each other (Titus 2).

viii. They promoted godliness in daily living: Titus was to teach different groups how to lead godly lives, how to adorn the teaching of Christ (Titus 2,3).

ix. They recognized the centrality of Gospel and Church in God's saving plan: Paul taught how believers are to live in the church (1 Timothy 3:15).

x. They were committed to prayer and suffering for the sake of the church: Paul instructed Timothy and Titus on how to reform the churches of their day, and called on them to join with him in suffering for the gospel (2 Timothy 1,2).

xi. They promoted Gospel outreach: Paul tells Timothy to do the work of an evangelist, and his aim was that the Gospel might be fully proclaimed, that all the nations might hear it (2 Timothy 4: 5, 17).

xii. They had a strategy of planning for the future: Paul encouraged Timothy and Titus to plan for future ministry in subsequent generations (2 Timothy 2:2, Titus 1: 5-9).[18]

Finally, trust the providential care of God, and his accomplishment of his gospel plan for the world, and don't judge those who make different decisions to yours. A number of years ago I decided that I would respect those who decided to stay in Anglican ministry even if it meant doing things I that could not do, and to respect those who left Anglican ministry for good reasons. I hope they will return the compliment!

Gospel trials should not be unexpected. They are a sign of the true church of God in every age. So the nonconformist

---

[18] Adam, 'Halfly Reformed', pp. 185-216.

Matthew Henry preached these words in 1706:

> It is no new thing for the church of Christ on earth to be in distress and bondage, and to stand in need of redemption, notwithstanding the great redemption from sin and hell, which the Lord Jesus has wrought out. It is always militant, it is often afflicted, tossed with tempests, and not comforted...[19]

And Henry Scougal preached a message of hope for those who are afflicted:

> There is nothing more acceptable unto God, no object more lively and amiable in His eyes, than a soul thus prostrated before Him, thus entirely resigned unto His holy will, thus quietly submitting to His most severe dispensations...Now, to this God who loves us, and corrects us for our profit, that we may be partakers of His holiness and thereby of His happiness; to God the Father, Son, and blessed Spirit, be all honour, praise and glory, now and forever. Amen.[20]

---

[19] Matthew Henry, *The Complete Works of Matthew Henry*, Vol. 1, (Grand Rapids: Baker, 1979 {1855}), p. 462.

[20] Scougal, *Works*, pp. 141-142.

6. Bibliography

Ackroyd, Peter, 'Strangers to Correction: Christian Discipline and the English Reformation', in Lee Gatiss, [ed.], *Preachers, Pastors and Ambassadors, The St Antholin's Lectures, Volume II, 2001-2010*, (London: The Latimer Trust, 2011), pp. 123-148.

Adam, Peter, 'Calvin's Preaching and Homiletic: Nine Engagements', Parts 1 and 2, *Churchman*, Vol. 124, Nos. 3 and 4, 2010.

Adam, Peter, '"Preaching of a Lively Kind": Calvin's engaged expository preaching', in *Engaging with Calvin. Aspects of the Reformer's legacy for today*, Mark D. Thompson [ed.], (Nottingham: Apollos, 2009).

Adam, Peter, 'A Church "Halfly Reformed": the Puritan Dilemma', republished in Lee Gatiss, [ed.], *Pilgrims, Warriors, and Servants, The St Antholin's Lectures, Volume I 1991-2000*, (London: The Latimer Trust, 2010), pp. 185-216.

Adam, Peter, 'The Scriptures are God's Voice: the Church is His Echo', in B.N. Kaye, [ed.], *Wonderfully and Confessedly Strange: Australian Essays in Anglican Ecclesiology*, (Hindmarsh: ATF Press, 2006), pp. 81-102.

Adam, Peter, 'To bring men to heaven by preaching: John Donne's Evangelistic Sermons', republished in Lee Gatiss, [ed.], *Preachers, Pastors, Ambassadors, The St Antholin's Lectures, Volume II, 2001-2010*, (London: The Latimer Trust, 2011), pp. 261-292.

Adam, Peter, 'Word and Spirit: the Puritan-Quaker Debate', in Lee Gatiss, [ed.], *Preachers, Pastors, Ambassadors, The St Antholin's Lectures, Volume II, 2001-2010*, (London: The Latimer Trust, 2011), pp. 49-96.

Adam, Peter, *The 'Very pure Word of God': the Book of Common Prayer as a model of Biblical Liturgy*, (London: The Latimer Trust, 2012).

Allison, C. Fitzsimmons, *The Rise of Moralism: the Proclamation of The Gospel from Hooker to Baxter*, (Wilton: Morehouse Barlow, 1966).

Anderson, Marvin W., *Evangelical Foundations: Religion in England, 1378-1683*, (New York: Lang, 1987).

Atherstone, Andrew, *Charles Simeon on "The Excellency of the Liturgy"*, (Norwich: Canterbury Press, 2012).

Avis, Paul, *Anglicanism and the Christian Church*, (Edinburgh: T&T Clark, 1989).

Baker, Frank, *William Grimshaw 1708-1763*, (London: Epworth Press, 1963).

Barker, William S., *Puritan Profiles*, (Fearn: Mentor, 1996).

Baxter, Richard, *A Christian Directory, Baxter's Practical Works Vol I*, Reprint, (Ligonier: Soli Deo Gloria, 1990 {nd}).

Baxter, Richard, *The Autobiography of Richard Baxter*, N.H Keeble [ed.], (London: Dent, 1974).

Bebbington, D. W., *Evangelicalism in Modern Britain: A History from the 1730s to the 1980s*, (London: Unwin Hyman, 1989).

Beeke, Joel R., 'Evangelicalism and the Dutch Further Reformation', in Michael A.G. Haykin and Kenneth J. Stewart, [eds.], *The Emergence of Evangelicalism: Exploring Historical Continuities*, (Nottingham: Apollos, 2008), pp. 146-168.

Benn, Wallace, 'Ussher on Bishops: A Reforming ecclesiology', in Lee Gatiss, [ed.], *Preachers, Pastors, Ambassadors: Puritan Wisdom for Today's Church, St Antholin's Lectures, Volume II, 2001-2010* (London: The Latimer Trust, 2011), pp. 97-122.

Bosher, Robert S., *The Making of the Restoration Settlement: The Influence of the Laudians: 1649-1662*, (Westminster: Dacre Press, 1951).

Bray, Gerald, [ed.], *Documents of the English Reformation*, (Minneapolis: Fortress Press, 1994).

Bray, Gerald, *The Faith We Confess*, (London: The Latimer Trust, 2009).

Bremer, Francis J., *The Puritan Experiment: New England Society from Bradford to Edwards*, (London: St James Press, 1976).

Buchanan, Colin, Lloyd, Trevor and Miller, Harold, [eds.], *Anglican Worship Today*, (London: Collins, 1980).

Bunting, Ian, ed., *Celebrating the Anglican Way*, (London: Hodder and Stoughton, 1996).

Burkitt, William, *Expository Notes, with Practical Observations on the New Testament of our Lord and Saviour Jesus Christ*, (Liverpool: Caxton, nd).

Calvin, John, *Come Out From Among Them: 'Anti-Nicodemite' Writings of John Calvin*, tr. Seth Skolnitsky, (Dallas: Protestant Heritage Press, 2001).

Carpenter, Edward, *The Protestant Bishop: Being the Life of Henry Compton, 1632-1713, Bishop of London*, (London: Longmans, 1956).

Carson, D.A. [ed.], *Worship by the Book*, (Grand Rapids: Zondervan, 2002).

Chadwick, Owen, *The Reformation*, (Harmondsworth: Penguin, 1972).

Cinnamond, Andrew, *What Matters in Reforming the Church? Puritan Grievances under Elizabeth I*, St Antholin Lectureship, (London: The Latimer Trust, 2011).

Cliffe, J.T., *Puritans in Conflict: The Puritan Gentry during and after the Civil Wars*, (London and New York: Routledge, 1988).

Collinson, Patrick, *Archbishop Grindal, 1519-1583: The Struggle for a Reformed Church*, (London: Jonathan Cape, 1979).

Collinson, Patrick, *The Elizabethan Puritan Movement*, (London: Jonathan Cape, 1967).

Collinson, Patrick, *The Religion of Protestants: The Church in English Society 1559-1625*, (Oxford: Clarendon Press, 1984).

Cragg, Gerald R., *From Puritanism to the Age of Reason: A Study of Changes in Religious thought within the Church of England 1660-1700*, (Cambridge: Cambridge University Press, 1966).

Cragg, Gerald R., *Puritanism in the period of the Great Persecution 1660-1688*, (Cambridge: Cambridge University Press, 1957).

Cragg, Gerald R., *The Church and the Age of Reason 1648-1789*, (Harmondsworth: Penguin, 1972).

Cressy, David, and Ferrell, Lori Anne, [eds.], *Religion and Society in Early Modern England: A Sourcebook*, (London and New York: Routledge, 1996).

Dallimore, Arnold, *George Whitefield: the life and times of the great evangelist of the 18th century revival*, Vol. 1, (London: Banner of Truth, 1970).

Davies, Julian, *The Caroline captivity of the church: Charles I and the Remoulding of Anglicanism 1625-1641*, (Oxford: Clarendon Press, 1992).

Dever, Mark, *Richard Sibbes: Puritanism and Calvinism in Late Elizabethan and Early Stuart England*, (Macon: Mercer University Press, 2000).

Dickens, A.G., *The English Reformation*, (London: Collins, 1967).

Doerksen, David W., *Conforming to the Word: Herbert, Donne, and the English Church before Laud*, (Lewisburg: Bucknell University Press/London: Associated University Presses, 1997).

Dugmore, C.W., *Eucharistic Doctrine in England from Hooker to Waterland*, (London: SPCK, 1942).

Durston, Christopher, and Eales, Jacqueline, [eds.], *The Culture of English Puritanism 1560-1700*, (Houndmills: Macmillan, 1996).

Evelyn, John, *The Diary of John Evelyn*, (London: Macmillan, 1906).

Ferguson, J.P., *Dr Samuel Clarke: An Eighteenth Century Heretic*, (Kineton: Roundwood, 1976).

Field, David, '"Decalogue" Dod and his Seventeenth Century Bestseller: a 400th Anniversary Appreciation', in Gatiss, Lee, [ed.], *Preachers, Pastors and Ambassadors, The St Antholin's Lectures, Volume II, 2001-2010*, (London: The Latimer Trust, 2011), pp. 149-204.

Field, David P., *'Rigide Calvinisme in a softer dresse': The Moderate Presbyterianism of John Howe, 1630-1705*, Rutherford Studies in Historical Theology, (Edinburgh: Rutherford House, 2004).

Fincham, Kenneth, *Prelate as Pastor: the Episcopate of James I*, (Oxford: Oxford University Press, 1990).

Fincham, Kenneth, *The Early Stuart Church 1603-1642*, (Stanford: Stanford University Press, 1993).

Gatiss Lee, *The Tragedy of 1662: The Ejection and Persecution of the Puritans*, Latimer Studies 66, (London: The Latimer Trust, 2007).

Gatiss, Lee, *The True Profession of the Gospel: Augustus Toplady and reclaiming our Reformed foundations*, (London: Latimer Trust, 2010).

Gatiss, Lee, [ed.], *Pilgrims, Warriors, and Servants, The St Antholin's Lectures, Volume I, 1991-2000*, (London: The Latimer Trust, 2010).

Gatiss, Lee, [ed.], *Preachers, Pastors and Ambassadors, The St Antholin's Lectures, Volume II, 2001-2010*, (London: The Latimer Trust, 2011).

Gatiss, Lee, *For Us and For Our Salvation: 'Limited Atonement' in Bible, Doctrine, History, Theology and Ministry*, (London: The Latimer Trust, 2012).

Gould, G. [ed.], *Documents Relating to the Settlement of the Church of England by the Act of Uniformity of 1662*, (London: Kent, 1862).

Green, I.M., *The Re-Establishment of the Church of England 1660-1663*, (Oxford: Oxford University Press, 1978).

Green, V.H.H., *Religion at Oxford and Cambridge*, (London: SCM, 1964).

Greschat, Martin, *Martin Bucer: A Reformer and his times*, (Louisville: Westminster John Knox, 2004).

Griffin, Martin I.J. Jr., *Latitudinarians of the Seventeenth Century Church of England*, (Leiden: Brill, 1992).

Hampton, Stephen, *Anti-Arminians: The Anglican Reformed Tradition from Charles II to George I*, (Oxford: Oxford University Press, 2008).

Harris, Tim, Seaward, Paul and Goldie, Mark, [eds.], *The Politics of Religion in Restoration England*, (Oxford: Blackwell, 1990).

Hart D.G. and Mueller, John R. [eds.], *With Reverence and Awe: Returning to the Basics of Reformed Worship*, (Philippsburg: P&R, 2002).

Haweis, Thomas, *The Evangelical Expositor, or Commentary on the Whole Bible...* (Glasgow: Somerville, Fullarton, Blackie, 1822).

Henry, Matthew, *The Complete Works of Matthew Henry*, Vol. 1, (Grand Rapids: Baker, 1979 {1855}).

Herbert, George, *The Works of George Herbert*, F.E. Hutchinson [ed.], (Oxford: Clarendon Press, 1941).

Hill, Christopher, *Puritanism and Revolution: Studies in Interpretation of the English Revolution of the 17th Century*, (London: Secker and Warburg, 1958).

Hill, Christopher, *Society and Puritanism in Pre-Revolutionary England*, (London: Panther, 1969).

Hill, Christopher, *A Turbulent, Seditious and Factious People: John Bunyan and his Church*, (Oxford: Oxford University Press, 1989).

Hill, Christopher, *The English Bible and the Seventeenth Century Revolution*, (London: Penguin, 1993).

Hopkins, Hugh Evan, *Charles Simeon of Cambridge*, (London: Hodder and Stoughton, 1977).

Hunt, Arnold, *The Art of Hearing: English preachers and their Audiences, 1590-1640*, (University of Cambridge PhD Thesis, 1998).

Hutton, Ronald, *The Restoration: A Political and Religious History of England and Wales 1658-1667*, (Oxford: Clarendon, 1985).

Hylson-Smith, Kenneth, *Evangelicals in the Church of England, 1734-1984*, (Edinburgh: T&T Clark, 1989).

Kimnach, W.H., Minkeema, K.P., and Sweeny, D.A., [eds.], *The Sermons of Jonathan Edwards: A Reader*, (New Haven and London: Yale University Press, 1999).

Knox, D.B., *The Thirty-Nine Articles: The historic basis of Anglican Faith*, (London: Hodder and Stoughton, 1967).

Lake, Peter, *Moderate Puritans and the Elizabethan Church*, (Cambridge: Cambridge University Press, 1982).

Lambert, Frank, *'Pedlar in Divinity': George Whitefield and the Transatlantic Revivals*, (Princeton: Princeton University Press, 1994).

Leighton, Robert, 'A Practical Commentary on the First Epistle General of St Peter', *The Whole Works of Robert Leighton*, Vol. I, J.N. Pearson [ed.], (London: James Duncan, 1835), pp. 109-609.

Linnell, Charles, *Some East Anglian Clergy*, (London: Faith Press, 1961).

Lloyd-Jones, D. Martyn [ed.], *Puritan Papers, Volume One, 1956-1959*, (Phillipsburg: P&R, 2001).

Lloyd-Jones, D. Martyn [ed.], *The Puritans: Their Origins and Successors, Addresses Delivered at the Puritan and Westminster Conferences, 1959-1978*, (Edinburgh: Banner of Truth, 1987).

MacCulloch, Dairmaid, *Building a Godly Realm: The Establishment of English Protestantism*, (London: The Historical Association, 1992).

MacCulloch, Diarmaid, *Reformation: Europe's House Divided 1490-1700*, (London: Penguin, 2004).

Marsden, George M., *Jonathan Edwards: A Life*, (New Haven: Yale University Press, 2003).

Marvell, Andrew, *Selected Poetry and Prose*, Robert Wilcher [ed.], (London: Methuen, 1986).

Matthews, A.G., *Calamy Revised*, (Oxford: Clarendon, 1988 {1934}).

McClelland, Joseph C., *The Visible Words of God: An Exposition of the Sacramental theology of Peter Martyr Vermigli, 1500-1562*, (Edinburgh: Oliver and Boyd, 1957).

McDonald, H. D., *Ideas of Revelation: An Historical Study A.D. 1700 to A.D. 1860*, (London: Macmillan, 1959).

Moule, H.C.G., *Charles Simeon*, (London: Inter-Varsity Fellowship, 1956).

Murray, Iain, [ed.], *Sermons of the Great Ejection*, (London: Banner of Truth, 1962).

Murray, Iain, [ed.], *The Reformation of the Church: A Collection of Reformed and Puritan Documents on Church Issues*, (Edinburgh: Banner of Truth, 1965).

Neill, C. and Willoughby, J. M., *The Tutorial Prayer Book*, (London: Church Book Room Press, 1959).

Null, Ashley, 'Thomas Cranmer and Tudor Evangelicalism', in Michael A.G. Haykin and Kenneth J. Stewart, [eds.], *The Emergence of Evangelicalism: Exploring Historical Continuities*, (Nottingham: Apollos, 2008), pp. 221-251.

Null, Ashley, *The Thirty-Nine Articles and Reformation Anglicanism*, (Mukono: Uganda Christian University, 2005).

Nuttall, Geoffrey F., and Owen Chadwick, *From Uniformity to Unity, 1662-1962*, (London: SPCK, 1962).

Nuttall, Geoffrey F., *Richard Baxter*, (London: Nelson, 1965).

Oden, Thomas, 'Do Not Rashly Tear Asunder: Why the Beleaguered Faithful should stay and reform their churches, *First Things*, April 2012, pp. 40-44.

O'Donovan, Oliver, *On the Thirty-Nine Articles: A Conversation with Tudor Christianity*, (Exeter: Paternoster Press, 1993).

Old, Hughes Oliphant, *The Reading and Preaching of the Scriptures in the Worship of the Christian Church, Volume 4, The Age of the Reformation*, (Grand Rapids and Cambridge: Eerdmans, 2002).

Overton, J.H. and Relton, F., *The English Church from the Accession of George I. to the end of the Eighteenth Century 1714-1800*, (London: Macmillan, 1906).

Owen, John, *The Works of John Owen, Volumes 13-15*, (London: Banner of Truth, 1966 {1850-53}).

Packer, J.I., [ed.], *Puritan Papers, Volume Two, 1960-1962*, (Phillipsburg: P&R, 2001).

Packer, J.I., *The Redemption and Restoration of Man in the Thought of Richard Baxter, Studies in Evangelical History and Thought*, (Carlisle: Paternoster, 2003).

Packer, James I., *The Thirty-Nine Articles: their Place and Use Today*, (London: Latimer Trust, 2006 {1984}).

Parker, T.H.L., *The Oracles of God: an Introduction to the Preaching of John Calvin*, (London and Redhill: Lutterworth, 1947).

Parker, T.H.L., *Calvin's Preaching*, (Edinburgh: T&T Clark, 1992).

Pearson, John, *An Exposition of the Creed*, W.S. Dobson [ed.], (London: Scott, Webster and Geary, 1842).

Pepys, Samuel, *The Shorter Pepys*, Robert Latham [ed.], (London: Folio, 1985).

Perkins, William, *The Art of Prophesying, The Calling of the Ministry*, (Edinburgh: Banner of Truth, 1996).

Poole-Connor, E.J., *Evangelicalism in England*, (Worthing: Walter, 1965).

Redwood, John, *Reason, Ridicule and Religion: The Age of Enlightenment in England 1660-1750*, (London: Thames and Hudson, 1976).

Robinson, Geoffrey, *The Tyrannicide Brief: The Story of the Man who sent Charles I to the Scaffold*, (London: Vintage, 2006).

Ryken, Leland, *Worldly Saints: The Puritans As They Really Were*, (Grand Rapids: Academie, 1990).

Ryle, J.C., *Knots Untied: being plan statements on disputed points in religion from the standpoint of an Evangelical Churchman*, (Cambridge: James Clarke, 1977).

Ryle, J.C., *Principles for Churchmen*, (London: C.J. Thynne, 1900).

Samuel, David, [ed.], *The Evangelical Succession in the Church of England*, (Cambridge: James Clarke, 1979).

Scougal, Henry, *The Works of Henry Scougal 1650-1678*, (Morgan: Soli Deo Gloria, 2002).

Seaver, Paul S., *The Puritan Lectureships*, (Stanford: Stanford University Press, 1970).

Smyth, Charles, *The Art of Preaching: 747-1939*, (London: SPCK, 1940).

Spencer, H. Leith, *English Preaching in the Late Middle Ages*, (Oxford: Clarendon, 1993).

Spurgeon, Charles Haddon, *Memories of Stambourne*, (Pasadena: Pilgrim, 1975).

Spurr, John, *English Puritanism, 1603-1689*, (Houndmills: Macmillan, 1998).

Spurr, John, *The Post-Reformation: Religion, Politics and Society in Britain 1603-1714*, (Harlow: Pearson Longman, 2006).

Spurr, John, *The Restoration Church of England, 1646-1689*, (New Haven and London: Yale University Press, 1991).

Sykes, Norman, *From Sheldon to Secker: Aspects of English Church History 1660-1768*, (Cambridge: Cambridge University Press, 1959).

Thomas, I.D.E., *A Puritan Golden Treasury*, (Edinburgh: Banner of Truth, 1977).

Thomas, Keith, *Religion and the Decline of Magic*, (London: Penguin, 1991).

Thomas, W.H. Griffith, *The Principles of Theology: An Introduction to the Thirty-Nine Articles*, (Oregon: Wipf and Stock Publishers, 2005).

Toon, Peter, *The Emergence of Hyper-Calvinism in English Nonconformity 1689-1765*, (London: Olive Tree, 1967).

Toplady, Augustus, *The Complete Works of Augustus Toplady*, (Harrisonburg: Sprinkle, 1987 {1794}).

Trueman, Carl R., *The Claims of Truth: John Owen's Trinitarian Theology*, (Carlisle: Paternoster, 1998).

Tyacke, N., *Aspects of English Protestantism, c.1530-1700*, (Manchester: Manchester University Press, 2001).

Underdown, David, *Fire from Heaven: The Life in an English Town in the Seventeenth Century*, (London: Pimlico, 2003).

Van Dixhorn, Chad B., 'A Puritan Theology of Preaching', in Gatiss, Lee, [ed.], *Preachers, Pastors and Ambassadors, The St Antholin's Lectures, Volume II, 2001-2010*, (London: The Latimer Trust, 2011), pp. 206-259.

Walker, F. Deaville, *William Carey, missionary pioneer and statesman*, (London: SCM, 1926).

Watson, Thomas, *A Body of Divinity*, (London: Banner of Truth, 1958).

Webster, Tom, *Godly Clergy in Early Stuart England: The Caroline Puritan Movement c1620-1643*, (Cambridge: Cambridge University Press, 1997).

Wesley, John, *The Journal of John Wesley, Volume Two*, Nehemiah Curnock [ed.], (London: Epworth Press, 1938).

White, James F. [ed.], *The Sunday Service of the Methodists in North America*, (Cleveland: OSL Publications, 1991).

Whitefield, George, *The Sermons of George Whitefield*, Parts 1 and 2, Lee Gatiss [ed.], (Watford: Church Society, 2010).

Willey, Basil, *The Seventeenth-Century Background*, (London: Penguin, 1962).

Withey, Donald A., *John Henry Newman: The Liturgy and the Breviary*, (London: Sheed and Ward, 1992).

Wood, A. Harold, *Church unity without uniformity: A Study of Seventeenth Century English Church Movements and of Richard Baxter's Proposals for a Comprehensive Church*, (London: Epworth, 1963).

Wood, Arthur Skevington, *Thomas Haweis 1734-1820*, (London: SPCK, 1957).

Zahl, Paul F. M., *The Protestant Face of Anglicanism*, (Grand Rapids/Cambridge: Eerdmans, 1998).

St. Antholin's Lectureship Charity Lectures

In or about 1559 the parish of St. Antholin, now absorbed into what is the parish of St Mary-le-Bow in Cheapside and St Mary Aldermanbury, within the Cordwainer's Ward in the City of London, came into the possession of certain estates known as the 'Lecturer's Estates.' These were, it is believed, purchased with funds collected at or shortly after the date of the Reformation for the endowment of lectures, mid-week sermons or talks by Puritan preachers.

Over the centuries the funds were not always used for the stated purpose, and in the first part of the nineteenth century a scheme was drawn up which revivified the lectureship, which was to consist of forty lectures to be given three times a year on the "Puritan School of Divinity", the lecturer to receive one guinea per lecture. A further onerous requirement was that the lecturer had to be a beneficed Anglican, living within one mile of the Mansion House in the City of London.

Under such conditions the lectureship fell into disuse a long time ago, and it was not until 1987 that moves were put in hand with the Charity Commissioners to update the scheme. The first lecture under the new scheme was given in 1991.

St. Antholin's Lectureship Charity Lectures

1991   J.I.Packer, *A Man for All Ministries: Richard Baxter 1651-1691.*

1992   Geoffrey Cox, *The Recovery and Renewal of the Local Church – the Puritan Vision.*

1993   Alister E. McGrath, *Evangelical Spirituality – Past Glories – Present Hopes – Future Possibilities.*

1994   Gavin J. McGrath, *'But We Preach Christ Crucified': The Cross of Christ in the Pastoral Theology of John Owen.*

1995   Peter Jensen, *Using the Shield of Faith – Puritan Attitudes to Combat with Satan.*

1996   J.I.Packer, *An Anglican to Remember – William Perkins: Puritan Popularizer.*

1997   Bruce Winter, *Pilgrim's Progress and Contemporary Evangelical Piety.*

1998   Peter Adam, *A Church 'Halfly Reformed' – the Puritan Dilemma.*

1999   J.I.Packer, *The Pilgrim's Principles: John Bunyan Revisited.*

2000   Ashley Null *Conversion to Communion: Thomas Cranmer on a Favourite Puritan Theme.*

2001   Peter Adam, *Word and Spirit: The Puritan-Quaker Debate.*

2002   Wallace Benn, *Usher on Bishops: A Reforming Ecclesiology.*

2003   Peter Ackroyd, *Strangers to Correction: Christian Discipline and the English Reformation.*

2004   David Field, *'Decalogue' Dod and his Seventeenth Century Bestseller: A Four Hundredth Anniversary Appreciation.*

2005   Chad B. Van Dixhoorn, *A Puritan Theology of Preaching.*

2006   Peter Adam, *'To Bring Men to Heaven by Preaching' – John Donne's Evangelistic Sermons.*

2007   Tony Baker, *1807 – 2007: John Newton and the Twenty-first Century.*

2008   Lee Gatiss, *From Life's First Cry: John Owen on Infant Baptism and Infant Salvation.*

2009   Andrew Atherstone, *Evangelical Mission and Anglican Church Order: Charles Simeon Reconsidered*

2010   David Holloway, *Re-establishing the Christian Faith – and the Public Theology Deficit.*

2011   Andrew Cinnamond, *What matters in reforming the Church? Puritan Grievances under Elizabeth I.*

2012   Peter Adam, *Gospel Trials in 1662: To stay or to go?*

Lightning Source UK Ltd.
Milton Keynes UK
UKOW051014020912

198343UK00001BA/14/P